Are we adequately preparing students for life beyond school doors? Schools teach students not to be competitive and never to fail. Yet in the real world, people compete for jobs and they often fail many times before reaching success. In this thought-provoking book, authors Johnson and Sessions describe 20 skills that are overlooked in schools and in educational standards but that are crucial to real-world success. They describe how you can develop these skills in your students, no matter what subject area or grade level you teach.

You'll learn how to

- promote leadership;
- allow competition;
- encourage meaningful engagement;
- help students find their voice;
- incorporate edutainment and pop culture;
- motivate towards excellence;
- hold students accountable and responsible;
- foster perseverance and the ability to learn from failure;
- teach effective communication;
- and much more!

Each chapter includes insightful research, thought-provoking stories, and practical strategies that you can take back to your own classroom.

Dr. Brad Johnson is an international speaker in the field of education. He has spent over 20 years in the education field, with experience as a teacher, curriculum director, and administrator. He earned a doctorate in curriculum studies from Georgia Southern University.

Dr. Julie Sessions has worked in education for 21 years. She is currently a fifth grade science teacher and Lower School curriculum coordinator at Porter-Gaud Sc

What Schools Don't Teach

20 Ways to Help Students Excel in School and Life

Brad Johnson and Julie Sessions

Routledge
Taylor & Francis Group

NEW YORK AND LONDON

First published 2015
by Routledge
711 Third Avenue, New York, NY 10017

and by Routledge
2 Park Square, Milton Park, Abingdon, Oxon OX14 4RN

Routledge is an imprint of the Taylor & Francis Group, an informa business

© 2015 Taylor & Francis

The right of Brad Johnson and Julie Sessions to be identified as authors of this work has been asserted by them in accordance with sections 77 and 78 of the Copyright, Designs and Patents Act 1988.

Library of Congress Cataloging-in-Publication Data
Johnson, Brad, 1969–
    What schools don't teach : 20 ways to help students excel in school and life /
Brad Johnson and Julie Sessions.
        pages cm
    Includes bibliographical references.
    1. Effective teaching.   2. School-to-work transition.   I. Sessions, Julie.   II. Title.
    LB1025.3.J586 2015
    371.102—dc23
    2014020154

ISBN: 978-1-138-80298-8 (hbk)
ISBN: 978-1-138-80340-4 (pbk)
ISBN: 978-1-315-75395-9 (ebk)

Typeset in Optima
by Apex CoVantage, LLC

Contents

Meet the Authors

Dr. Brad Johnson is an international speaker in the field of education. He is author of *The Edutainer: Connecting the art and science of teaching* and *Scared skinny no more: Exposing the myths of weight bias and weight loss*. Dr. Johnson has spent over 20 years in the education field, with experience as a teacher, curriculum director, and administrator. He is a leading expert in mentoring and leadership. He has written or contributed to numerous articles as an education expert for magazines including *Education World, Education Digest*, and *Teacher Gazette*. He currently teaches a graduate course in "Ethics of Leadership." Dr. Johnson has also coached athletes at the high school and collegiate level. He recently spent time in Malaysia developing a fitness diploma with their Ministry of Education. Dr. Johnson is represented by multiple speaking bureaus.

Dr. Julie Sessions has played many roles in education throughout her 21 years in public and private schools in the Charleston area. She has taught in grades 2–7, been a curriculum coordinator, chaired grade levels as well as departments, chaired and co-chaired reaccreditation committees, presented at numerous conferences, served on administrative search committees and lead teacher development. Dr. Sessions earned her undergraduate degree in elementary education with a specialty in literature, a master's degree in Reading from the Citadel, and obtained her certification as a reading diagnostician and reading specialist. She earned her doctorate of education in curriculum studies from Georgia Southern. Dr. Sessions is currently a fifth grade science teacher and Lower School curriculum coordinator at Porter-Gaud School in Charleston, South Carolina. She is married to Derek and has two boys, AJ and Ed.

For more information about Dr. Johnson, Dr. Sessions, the book, or speaking availability, please visit www.premiereleaders.com

Acknowledgments

We would like to thank the following people for sharing their time, expertise, and talents to help make this book possible: Elizabeth Berger (nationally recognized child psychologist), Doug Bergman (Microsoft Expert Educator, Porter-Gaud Computer Science Department Chair), Sarah Davis (reCreate leadership), Jennifer Fore (reCreate leadership), Deborah Gilboa (international parenting expert), Amanda Flisher (reCreate leadership), Amanda Kraus (Executive Director of Row New York), Diane Johnson May (Vice President of Human Resources, Kraft Food Groups), Jeff Lyle Johnson (artist), Christen Manari (Eduspire Ipad Instructor), Caroline Silby (nationally recognized sports psychologist).

"A recent graduate at his first job interview."

A School Picture

Introduction

" It is, in fact, nothing short of a miracle that the modern methods of education have not yet entirely strangled the holy curiosity of inquiry."

Albert Einstein

What is the purpose of formal education? Is it to do well on a standardized test? Is it to get accepted into college and procure a well-paying job? While those may be of some importance, we believe the primary focus of formal education should be to produce functional, capable members of society in all walks of life. The purpose of education should be to prepare students for life beyond school, whether it is college or the job market. It should also prepare students for a meaningful life and help them develop skills to become productive members of society.

If you noticed, we didn't limit it to just college preparation, which seems to be the only goal of education. However, the reality is a large portion of students will never attend college, much less graduate, so you can see that a focus only on college preparation is leaving most children unprepared for the real world. However, EVERY STUDENT deserves the opportunity to develop their talents and life skills, which will provide the best opportunity for them to EXCEL in life.

There have been many influential people from around the globe who have seen formal education as a hindrance to learning, if not downright harmful to students. Winston Churchill hated school and said he was filled with nothing but anxiety while attending school. Richard Branson dropped out of high school, and even Albert Einstein himself dropped out of high school. If these highly successful people felt this way about formal education, think of how millions of others feel about it as well.

Perhaps Benjamin Franklin said it best when describing the effect of education by remarking, *"He was so learned that he could name a horse in nine languages; so ignorant that he bought a cow to ride on."* This humorous quote pretty much sums up education to some extent. While we provide knowledge for students, we don't provide them with the ability to apply that knowledge to the real world. How many students do you know who graduate from high school, but have no idea what they really want to do? Beyond the big picture ideas, they also don't know how to buy a car, balance a checkbook, handle an irritating boss, or even cope with the stress of relationships.

What if education was looked at differently? What if students were given the coping skills to work for a boss they didn't like? What if students could effectively communicate with family, friends, and colleagues? What if teachers motivated students to find their passions while inspiring creativity, promoting teamwork, boosting self-reliance, and instilling excellence? What if students could identify and build on their leadership strengths?

Public education claims to value diversity, the individuality of each student, and even choice. In reality, education values testing and making sure all students act and think alike. Students are conditioned to move through an assembly-line of rules and testing. There is little opportunity given to develop their decision-making skills or provide choices where they feel ownership in the educational process. Individual differences, such as abilities, skills, passions, and strengths are also lost in the process. Ironically over one-fourth of students globally still don't even graduate high school, but education continues with the same assembly-line mentality. Those who do graduate are often unprepared for college and lack the skills to excel in the global economy.

So what ever happened to the pursuit of excellence and innovation in education? The skills to excel in the real world are not easily measured on a test and are often left out. Just because these skills cannot be measured on a test doesn't mean they aren't important. These are the skills described in *What Schools Don't Teach* which include creativity, leadership, flexibility, passion, vigor, teamwork, and more. This doesn't mean a skill such as reading is not important. In fact we discuss how to get boys more involved with reading, but passion is just as important to success. Counting is a skill that all students need, but character is just as important when it comes to being a productive citizen.

Every child is born with desires, strengths, and untapped potential. Not every student will be a teacher or even want to attend college. However, every child starts out wanting to be successful in life. Ironically, students who tend to do well in school and beyond are students who are not always rated the brightest, but those who work hard at achieving their personal goals. This is due in large part to the skills they develop such as competition, work ethic, and teamwork that aren't typically developed in the classroom.

The strategies in this book are a compilation of over forty years of experience between the two of us in K–12 education and the collegiate level. It also includes several years of coaching athletes from park and recreation through Division I collegiate athletes. We have identified and quantified many skills that are incorporated into sports, the arts, and other extracurricular activities that best demonstrate the skills needed for the real world. These are skills that are also transferable to the classroom. However, we concluded that most schools fail to develop many of these real-world skills needed by students to become productive members of society as well, focusing instead on preparing students for simply more testing.

Included in this book are many tips and ideas from real-world application that are not typical of most schools' curricula or teacher development books. Each chapter is divided into an easy-to-read format consisting of four sections which include some research, personal stories, ideas to implement in the classroom, and then key points to remember.

Teachers will appreciate that these strategies don't add more work but rather they can easily be incorporated into your curriculum to make it more effective. These strategies will create a learning environment where classroom behavior will improve, student engagement will increase, and students will find learning relevant and beneficial to their lives. This book takes learning to a level that will prepare students to excel not only in the classroom but in the real world.

Promote Leadership

" The function of leadership is to produce more leaders, not more followers."

Ralph Nader

Our Thoughts and Some Research Too

I (Brad) would like to start off this section with a question. Do you see your students as leaders? If so, then what talents or strengths do you think they possess that are leadership skills? Don't worry, this isn't a quiz but hopefully it does raise the question of how many people really understand leadership. The reality is that everyone has the potential to be a leader. We are all born with talents or traits that can be developed into effective leadership skills. But developing these skills has not been a priority of education or society in general. In fact maybe the first question I should ask is, as teacher or parent, are you aware of your leadership skills? Do you know what leadership skills you possess? And if you are aware of them, do you maximize those strengths in your professional and personal life?

The development of leadership skills in students is almost nonexistent. It is often neglected because realistically, we are educating our students to follow, not to lead. Think about it, in the typical school day, we train students to follow directions, follow a schedule, follow a straight line, and follow the 20 rules on the classroom wall, but when do we ever focus on leading? Everyone is aware that leadership is an essential quality for the real world; however, it is usually not a priority when it comes to students. In fact, rather than producing more leaders as the quote above suggests, we seem to be focused only on producing followers. Learning to be a follower is not a bad thing, but the problem arises when we teach students only to follow.

I asked earlier if you knew your own talents and leadership strengths. Sadly most adults are not aware of their own leadership strengths, much less how to help students develop their own leadership skills. Developing and utilizing your own strengths in your professional life will result in much higher job satisfaction and productivity. Research by Gallup indicates that when adults are able to use their strengths in their careers, then they are six times more likely to be engaged in their jobs and three times more likely to report having an excellent quality of life.

By contrast, studies show when people work in jobs where their strengths aren't utilized, they are not emotionally engaged in their jobs. Sadly, two-thirds of respondents don't feel like their strengths are utilized in their jobs. This means two-thirds of adults are not fully engaged in their work, have lower productivity, and do not view themselves as having an excellent quality of life. When students' leadership traits are discovered, developed, and utilized, they will be exponentially more successful in their careers, more productive, and this will carry over into their personal lives as well.

Unfortunately, in education and in society, we focus more on improving areas of weaknesses rather than developing strengths or leadership abilities. As leadership expert Sarah Davis explains, "The conventional approach is about maintaining an individual's strengths and work on fixing weaknesses. It's about identifying improvement areas and developing an improvement plan." You have to look no further than any job performance review or teacher observation to see that our approach is all about "fixing" weaknesses. While it is all right to improve areas of growth, the focus is never on developing our talents or strengths. However, she explains, "Instead we should focus on strengths, while also managing any weaknesses . . .. It's really about identifying a person's talents and developing them into strengths." So, imagine the strengths that we leave underdeveloped in our students.

Talents are our natural aptitudes or skills which, when developed become our **strengths**. The use and development of these strengths allow us to produce positive/successful outcomes. There are five traits or talents that are considered key components of leadership. These include intelligence, integrity, determination, self-confidence, and sociability. Being able to identify one or more of these traits within students is the starting point. From there, these skills need to be developed and encouraged to grow to become leadership qualities. Beyond these five traits there are also traits that many recognize as being innate. These include body size, intelligence, honesty, the ability to inspire, charisma, self-confidence, and even ambition. While these can be traits we are born with, it doesn't mean that they are fully developed at birth. Take, for instance, the example of body size. Arnold Schwarzenegger was born with great genetics, but he had to develop those genetics to reach his potential. He did not become seven-time Mr. Olympia simply because of his raw talent, but he had to train hard and develop his strengths to optimize his potential. On the other hand, what if he had decided to be a marathon runner? He could have trained hard, but his large frame would have never been advantageous to long distance running. He never would have been a world-class runner because it wasn't part of his strengths.

Another example may be a student in your classroom who possesses the positivity trait. You know the child, the one who is always encouraging others and making the best of every situation. These are people who always see the glass half full. Well guess what, that can be cultivated into a leadership skill. Would you rather work for an administrator who is positive, energetic, and always encouraging you? Or would you rather work for someone who only appears when there is a problem and only communicates what needs to be fixed? You know the type; they look like they are always sucking on a lemon. Which would you rather choose as a leader? Yet, if their enthusiasm and optimism are stifled because the teacher only has time to cover items for the test, then we aren't helping develop their strengths.

Fortunately, you don't need a formal assessment to recognize some of the leadership traits that your students possess. Students who seem to thrive on achievement or competition are the ones we tend to recognize because they seem to stand out. But what about the students in your class who love to tell stories and be the center of attention? Instead of cultivating these traits, we want them to sit down and be quiet. What about the student who is highly inquisitive? They always want to know who, what, where, when, how, and why. Yet, in our fast paced educational world, we usually only have time for the what before we move on to another standard. Or even the student who is good at making and maintaining friendships? Do we recognize and help develop these traits? Typically, the answer is no.

Being a leader also means knowing how to deal with adversity. People often become confrontational and feel that their voice is not being heard. A leader must know how to listen to everyone and be able to make everyone feel valued. Confrontation is an area in which all students and most adults can improve skills. Females tend to shy away, boys are taught that as well. A good leader can help others to learn how to properly deal with issues. They can help others to see that it's about the issues, not the individuals. Once the issues are the focus then they can be resolved. Peer mediation is a perfect example of this. With peer mediation the mediator, or leader, facilitates the listening to both sides and helps all of the parties involved feel validated, but also the focus is on the issues and not the people. By going through the peer mediation process, all people involved feel that they are a part of the solution. By having ownership in the solution the people have buy-in and will more than likely be able to resolve the problem. Being a leader during a peer mediation session takes training and skills, the type of skills that are sought in the job market today.

These types of concepts help alleviate issues in the classroom such as bullying. Bullying is not an issue that is corrected with a lesson or workbook on bullying, but it has to do with the respect and value that students place upon each other and themselves. Students who work together towards similar goals while respecting each other's differences and feelings will be better teammates and leaders. A good leader will not bully or will not allow bullying to take place within the group. The leader will lead by example and model respect and in turn expect respect among the teammates. If not, then a peer mediation process can take place. A leader always keeps everyone's feelings in mind and encourages the team to meet the set goal.

Remember there is an array of talents which students may possess. Some of these may not even seem like they are strengths, but when developed they can help students be more successful. Some of these talents include confidence, organization, the passion to discover, dependability, the ability to relate, team building, and risk taking. When these talents are identified and developed then they become strengths which help students maximize their potential. Students would improve their professional and personal relationships exponentially; allowing them to enhance their opportunities for success and improve every area of their lives.

Did you know?

US businesses spend around $14 billion dollars annually on leadership development because students aren't entering the world prepared to be leaders. www.bersin.com/blog/post/2012/07/Boosted-Spend-on-Leadership-Development-e28093-The-Facts-and-Figures.aspx

Personal Experiences and Stories

The lack of leadership development in our schools really resonated with me (Brad) during my first year of teaching leadership courses at the graduate level. My students were professionals in the field of education who were seeking their master's degree in leadership/administration. The course I teach focuses on developing leadership strengths. The feedback I have received from the students was an eye opener. Many students confess that they had never focused on what they do well (strengths) but had always been taught to work on the weaknesses. Almost unanimously they say this course is the most useful and helpful college course they have ever taken. Remember these are teachers and teacher leaders with 10, 15, and even 20 years of experience in education. Most of them had never thought about having leadership strengths, much less having them utilized by their administrators. If their talents/strengths aren't being maximized, how do we expect students to maximize their abilities? What I find ironic is that we expect to develop transformational leaders for the next generation, when the leaders of this generation have never fully developed their own leadership skills.

Therefore, we even miss the opportunity to fully develop the leadership potential of teachers because the focus has been on developing followers, not leaders. Remember the teacher observation I mentioned earlier? What is typically the focus of it? You guessed it, areas of growth or improvement. Very little attention is given to what teachers do well and where their strengths might be best suited and/or developed. Here is one more interesting bit of information that may help you rethink how we ourselves lead and especially how we develop leadership in our students. People are nearly 100 percent actively engaged in their jobs when their administration/managers focus upon their strengths. When the focus is on improving weaknesses or areas of growth, then the number drops to 78 percent of people who are actively engaged. Even worse is when administrators/managers ignore their employees, such as with poor management. Then only 60 percent of employees are actively engaged in their work.

These statistics remind me of the mother who had difficulty getting her son up every morning for school. Each morning she would have to call him multiple times to wake up. One morning she had had enough and stormed into his room and yelled at him to wake up. Her son said, "I hate school! The students make fun of me and the teachers don't like me!" He said, "Give me one good reason why I should go to school?" The mother looked at him and said I will give you two good reasons . . . number one you need to go because school is very important, and number two . . . you're the principal!"

This story always gets an eruption of laughter when I share it at conferences, but it does reinforce the point that leadership is important. If the principal didn't like school, can you imagine the environment he created for his teachers and even students? A lack of leadership skills affects everyone in an organization!

A good example of how to develop leadership in the classroom involves my science class where we use groups to conduct labs and do activities. All students have the opportunity to experience all of the different jobs within the lab setting at some point throughout the year. I make a point of telling the job expectations for each group member before each lab or activity. Students are able then to rate themselves as well as teammates in regards to how well they did in particular jobs. Even though everyone will do each job, there are times when I let them choose the one they feel strongest in in order to further develop those skills. They continue to gain confidence and become even better in an area that they already succeed in and enjoy. They are becoming masters, or leaders, of that particular job.

Earlier this year when I (Julie) was reviewing the expectations of a leader, I had a student raise his hand just as I was beginning my discourse. I stopped and asked if he had something to share. The student explained that he saw a poster the day before at his mom's work and thought of science class. It had two pictures, one on top of the other. The top picture was of a man standing to the side and yelling at people to pull a cart. The second was a picture of a man pulling along with the others and yelling in encouragement. He said the poster was about leadership. The class was silent and seemed to hang on every word he said. He ended the explanation by saying, "So, I think we should be the kind of leaders that pull the cart with our group's members and encourage each other." All I could do was nod with a smile on my face. I said that was a better explanation than I was about to give. I thanked him and asked if I could use that example in the other classes that day. It was obvious that this particular student already had leadership qualities because he could recognize what it took to be a good role model. I knew that would be a position he would grow in throughout the year. I truly feel that by allowing students to experience being leaders in a safe environment, such as a classroom, that it will help them to become leaders within the community and among their peers.

Did you know?

People who focus on their strengths rather than their weaknesses are less frustrated and exponentially more successful. http://workinginsync. com/category/team-dynamics

Ideas to Try

- **Hand-writing activity**: This activity allows kids to experientially compare a strengths-based approach versus a conventional approach. This activity is provided by ReCreate, a strengths based company.

    1. For this activity, take out a piece of paper and draw a line down the middle of the page.
    2. Choose a statement for kids to write like, "I use my talents every day."
    3. Tell them the activity will be timed and to raise their hand as soon as they complete the assignment. (**End clock once last student has completed task.)
    4. Instruct them on the left-hand side to write the phrase – "I use my talents everyday" with their NON-DOMINANT HAND.
    5. Time class.
    6. Once completed with non-dominant hand instruct them now to write the same phrase "I use my talents everyday" with their DOMINANT hand.
    7. Time class.
    8. Ask the class how Round 1 felt. You should hear comments like "weird," "hard," "awkward."
    9. Ask the class how Round 2 felt. You should hear comments like "nothing," "fine," "normal."
    10. Ask the class about the: Quality between the 2 rounds? Consistency between the 2 rounds? Ask them what the point of this activity might be?

The Responses:

This is what it feels like to work at something using our greatest talents vs. using your lesser talents. Round 1 felt awkward. You could do it but think about how much effort and time it took and how poor the quality was. We need to start working from our innate talents and focus on those vs working at our lesser talents which will never be as good as what comes so naturally to you.

- **Interest inventory or leadership assessment survey**: Help children build their leadership self-confidence by giving them opportunities to do things in which they can be successful. The key here is to understand their strengths and let them develop those strengths. Having the students complete an interest inventory or leadership assessment survey will help to find these strengths. For example, you may have a student who is not one of your top achievers academically, however they may be competitive, so create activities that incorporate some level of competition which will engage the student and give them a more positive experience.

- **Identify characteristics and example of traits**: Choose traits that correlate with leadership and have students identify characteristics or examples of performing these traits. For example, write the following traits on the board: intelligence, integrity, determination, self-confidence, and sociability. Then have the students brainstorm meanings and examples of the words in relation to your classroom. Then have them make connections to real life. Finally, have them rate themselves in each category to find out which ones they think they excel in and which ones they are interested in. From there, give them opportunities to experience growth and success in those areas.

- **Communicating opportunities**: Good communication is a key component to being an effective leader. Teach children how to listen carefully and how to respond to others in a calm and respectful way. Teaching children to negotiate is another effective communication tool as well. A great opportunity for students to develop their communication skills is by public speaking. During my years in the classroom, I have always had students present projects and reports to the whole class. This makes them comfortable speaking in front of audiences, but it also allows them the opportunity to work on skills such as maintaining eye contact, speaking with a projected voice, and working on nonverbal skills as well. I also have sharing time in class with what I call a 1-2-1 concept. This is where students share for one minute uninterrupted and then the class can ask two questions and provide one comment. Students learn to listen carefully and then to ask meaningful questions and comments. They love the time they have to share and the short time period gets them used to talking in front of peers and being concise and to the point.

- **Teamwork**: Teach children how to work with others in a team situation such as group projects or sports activities. Compromise and teamwork are important leadership qualities that allow students to see the big picture, not just their perspective. Allowing them to assume various roles when working on a team project will help them see these other perspectives and learn to not only compromise, but also effectively communicate.

- **Problem solving**: Find ways to create problem-solving situations. Allow children to start making small decisions such as picking which activity they want to participate in. Think outside the box and include activities that can allow their different strengths to be utilized. Think of activities that may utilize cooperation, adaptability, competition, responsibility, or even strategy. The key is to allow different students to either find or develop their strengths. Our grade level has about 70 students who go to recess at the same time. While there are numerous areas to play, there is only one big field. Our first problem-solving task of the year is setting up a schedule for the field so that everyone can play a sport of their choice at some time. This process takes several class meetings, but in the end turns out to be so much more effective than any schedule a teacher could have created. The students not only have ownership in the idea, but also in the process it took to create the final schedule.

- **Build self-confidence**: The thought of "leadership" can be overwhelming, even to adults. So, give the students many opportunities to develop their strengths so they are comfortable with the idea of leadership. Also, break down activities or tasks so they are manageable and achievable. Success in developing strengths will provide students with self-confidence, which happens to be an important leadership trait. The students often do not have self-confidence and at times feel bad for succeeding in a task. I have had some students who do not want to showcase good grades because they are embarrassed. We need to recognize this and help them build self-confidence in a meaningful way. Being self-confident does not equate with bragging and putting others down. This needs to be taught! Students, and even adults, do not always know how to do this respectfully. Use as many opportunities as possible to help students recognize when students are developing their strengths. Also use examples that would show the difference between being self-confident and just plain out rude and bragging. Once the students see these examples then they will be able to recognize them and positively show their self-confidence.

- **Social skills**: Allow students to develop their social skills. This sounds counterintuitive to most schools where students are expected to sit still at a desk all day long. However, sociability is not only an important leadership skill, it is an important skill for every role and relationship in which we exist. This can be structured social interaction as simple as a name game, charades, guessing facial expressions, to more complex interactions such as improvised group story telling or creating a play and acting it out in class.

- **Identify leaders**: Have students identify leaders in the real world within your area of study, town, city, country, and around the world. What leadership qualities do the students recognize and identify with? Is it a sports figure, an actor, a politician, a parent? Create lessons that help the students recognize the qualities of the leaders that were identified and then have them make personal connections to their own qualities that they possess. In science class we first identify leaders within the scientific community (Newton, Galileo, Einstein) and then branch out and have students identify other leaders that have had an impact in history. We then continue with other categories that they brainstorm, which usually includes music, sports, and movies. These types of lessons help make connections to the real world and help them identify leadership qualities in many different genres.

- **Risk taking**: One characteristic of most leaders is the willingness to take risk. This doesn't mean reckless risks, but more often calculated risks. Demonstrate risk taking in the classroom or share examples of risk taking. For instance, I always shared with my students the first time I went snow skiing. I took lessons and spent most of my time on the "bunny slope." But by the end of the day I was going down one of the easy runs. However, I wiped out several times during the day. If I had stayed on the bunny slope, I might not have fallen, but I wouldn't have really improved. It was learning to balance and adjust as I was falling which helped me improve the most. Creating a safe environment for risk taking is important as well.

Key Points to Remember

- Define and give examples of what leadership means.

- Help students identify their talents and develop them into strengths (such as leadership assessments or inventories).

- Model leadership qualities. Modeling is an effective way to enhance any skills.

- Give students the opportunity to be leaders (group work, teamwork, peer mediation, etc.).

- Share examples outside the classroom of positive and negative leaders and lead discussion with the students why they are/are not effective leaders.

- Have leadership skills posted in the classroom.

- Give them assignments or problems to solve without guiding the process of completing the goal. Allow students to utilize their strengths in the group and problem-solve themselves. This will give them a sense of engagement and accomplishment.

2 | **Allow Competition**

" I have been up against tough competition all my life. I wouldn't know how to get along without it. "

Walt Disney

Our Thoughts and Some Research Too

If there is one word I would use to describe humans, I think it is be competitive. From the beginning of time, humans have competed over resources, relationships, and religion. Just look at any family with siblings and you will see competition at its best (or maybe worst). Siblings compete over attention, the last piece of cake, and even time in the bathroom. Competition is what allows us to survive as a species. In fact, in the book, *Top Dog: The Science of Winning and Losing*, the authors examine competition from all angles – physiological, psychological, and historical. Their main point is that competition, if done right, is a good thing. In fact, competition and team activities can drive learning and performance better than solo endeavors. As they point out, siblings are involved in some type of competition with each other three or four times per hour. Since we know competition exists, why not help cultivate competitive skills rather than shying away from them.

Unfortunately, some psychologist and educational "experts" believe that competition in the classroom is a bad thing. They say that it can hurt self-esteem and has no place in the classroom. What they fail to understand is that success in today's school culture is defined by standardized tests, which by their nature are competitive. High stakes testing and the anxiety created by them are felt by all students both males and females.

Are students really prepared for high stakes testing when competition is discouraged in the classroom? No! So, to expect students to perform at a competitive level and then discourage competition is counterproductive. No wonder so many students feel anxiety and ill prepared for high stake testing.

Even beyond standardized testing, competition is an important part of life beyond the classroom. College admission is very competitive. The job market, especially in this fragile economy, is becoming increasingly competitive. Over one billion people have risen from poverty to the middle class around the globe in the last decade. These people are now competing for jobs in a global economy. Within the US economy, job growth is scarce and declining in some areas, so competition for jobs is greater than it has been in decades.

Competition is actually hardwired into our DNA (survival of the fittest). Have you ever wondered why boys enjoy video games so much? Part of it is entertaining, but in a culture where students have limited opportunities to compete, it provides an outlet for competition. One common theme among cultures around the world is the rite of passage of a boy into manhood. During the late nineteenth and early twentieth century, Britain actually developed sports programs in their schools as a way to prepare their young men to run the British Empire. There is now a renewed emphasis on sports in schools within the UK. After the 2012 Olympics, Prime Minister David Cameron said, "Bringing back competitive sports for primary pupils will help rid schools of their 'bureaucratic and anti-risk' culture." So, Mr. Cameron promised to put competitive sports such as netball and football into the national curriculum for primary school children.

In the US, team sports such as American football and baseball have become rites of passage for young men. They want to be like their heroes, who are often athletes themselves. In the UK and other countries these rites of passage include football (soccer), cricket, and other sports. Yet these same boys are expected to spend most of their waking hours in school, seated at a desk with little or no opportunity to engage in competitive activities.

With little opportunity for competition in schools, or lack of opportunity within the community, many find an outlet in video games. Think of how many hours a boy can spend trying to reach the next level of a game or playing online against friends. How long would they play these games if there was no competition involved? "Historically games have really been a lot about shoot 'em up sports, these are very aggressive activities. They're very competitive," said Lisa Leyba, the Senior Product Manager at Electronic Arts. Even with youth sports, where over 12 million boys participate, how many boys do you think would be interested in sports if there were no score kept? And then we wonder why students, especially males, claim that school is boring and uninteresting. Think of the decline in behavior issues and the dropout rate if boys felt this important aspect of their genetic makeup was being developed rather than stifled in the classroom.

However, this isn't just a male characteristic, but many females exhibit this as well. Female athletes who have been exposed to competitive sports also have a desire for competition. And research shows that female participation in athletics is on the rise. More than 8 million (ages 8–18) females participate in sports. Some may think that the increase is parental pressure, but this isn't the case. The majority of females name their coaches and physical education teachers mentors who have encouraged them in sports, rather than their parents.

Research also shows that by a 3–1 ratio, female athletes do better in school, do not drop out, and have a better chance to get through college. This is due in large part to the skills they develop such as competition, work ethic, and teamwork that aren't developed in the classroom. As the number of female athletes continue to rise, a lack of competition in the classroom will make school boring and uninteresting to these females, too. There is even a G.A.M.E.S. (Girls Advancing Math, Engineering, & Science) initiative to create video games that will increase the interest of girls in math and science. There are three specific games in development which are expected to be released in 2016.

Competition is not limited to sports either. When students participate in band, chorus, drama, and other extracurricular activities, they are exposed to competition as well. Even the National Spelling Bee attracts nearly 10 million students per year, with students competing for $50,000.00 in scholarship money at the televised finals.

Competition doesn't have to be the central theme of the classroom, but it needs to be incorporated into the learning process. While competition at the elementary level may not be as important as later years, it can still be included as a secondary or tertiary objective. Competition should become more of a focus as students enter high school where they feel the pressure to pass tests, prepare for college or jobs. Students who leave school without experiencing competition are at a disadvantage to students who have developed competitive skills. If you talk to athletes, musicians or any type of performers, they tend to get just as anxious and stressed out as novices but they interpret it differently. They see it as beneficial. They recognize that a little bit of butterflies or that little bit of tension, adrenaline, are all getting them ready for the moment where they concentrate and they focus and they associate that feeling with some of their greatest performances.

Competition doesn't have to single out any one student either. Competition can be successful with teams, groups, or even by grade level. There are life skills that can be developed through competition as well. By working together to achieve something, most competitions mean we need to work effectively with other people. This improves our communication skills, our socializing skills and all round ability to understand and work with other people. If children never experience losing or failure then they will have an unrealistic expectation of "I'm entitled to win" when they enter the real world. One other aspect that many teachers may find beneficial is that students who perform lower academically may be more willing to participate and stay on task if there are activities that involve competition such as Trash Basketball, which is described at the end of this section.

Finally, remember to encourage healthy competition which is beneficial to males and females. According to Amanda Kraus, Executive Director of Row New York (a program that helps youth from under-resourced communities build skills through the sport of rowing), "Sadly, young women are encouraged to compete around looks, attention from boys, their clothing (is it stylish or ugly?), when those focuses are all wrong. We should encourage competition around things the girls can actually control. That's why sports work so well. Sports hold up a mirror to the amount of work a girl puts in. Work hard and see results. Work together and go faster (in rowing). Delay gratification and see results (i.e. instead of sitting on the couch afterschool, get on the rowing machine and work out). These are the life lessons that take us places. If we can increase girls' comfort levels with competition (in healthy environments), we can make sure they enter college and careers with a good sense of trying their hardest and not being afraid to PUSH, to FAIL, to TRY AGAIN."

Students are not properly educated if they have not been given an opportunity to develop their competitive skills. It will leave them at a disadvantage in high stakes testing as well as the competitive global economy. Too many times we seem to be in situations where "everyone gets a trophy" and everyone wins. It is OK to learn how to lose, too. It is a part of life that is unavoidable and can even help us grow. But it's also important for the adults to offer competition in a healthy and supportive manner. As Ms. Kraus explains, adults should continually ask themselves if the students involved feel supported, are they rewarded for their good efforts, regardless of outcome. Are they being pushed to compete in a healthy way? Win, lose, or draw, competition should be a positive experience.

> ### *Did you know?*
>
> By adding competition to schools it brings BOTH the students and the teachers to higher levels of thinking. http://legacy.teachersfirst.com/gifted/strategies.html

Personal Experiences and Stories

Games are fun to play and can be a simple way to plug competition into units. But, can you take it a step further and bring competition into the curriculum? Let the students design their own games. Students who can teach content have mastered that content. There are numerous ways to have students create their own games, and they can even be a part of the final assessment taken by the teacher. In my fifth grade science class (students' average age 9–10) we use a program designed by MIT called SCRATCH. The students write codes to create a video game.

One specific assignment I (Julie) have designed is that the students must use 15 vocabulary words where the Sprites (characters) must interact with each other to show they understand the vocabulary terms. For example, a shark may swim towards a smaller fish and ask if it can eat it. The fish would be coded to respond yes because the shark is a carnivore. There are ways to add scoring to the games. One student asked trivia questions about the vocabulary terms and had the game coded that if the answer is correct then points are given and if the answers are incorrect then points are deducted. The majority of the students, both boys and girls want to add scoring to the game. It is amazing to watch other students play the games until they master all of the content and get a perfect score! If the games meet all requirements then they can be published on the Scratch website and the students have a published game. In this aspect the students are competing with the game or themselves and will play over and over to obtain their goal score.

I have taught students ranging from 7 years old to 16 years old and one thing that they all have in common is the love of playing games. I can think of examples in every age group and every subject area (I have taught science, English, social studies, reading, language arts, and math) where students have asked to play games in class. From the crazy review games, to silly games to learn vocabulary terms to games that teach math concepts to games that earn points towards an activity, the students ask for, often beg, for the chance to compete with and against one another.

The competition that I foster within my classroom is healthy where everyone has the opportunity to succeed at one time or another. Students learn to win and they learn to lose. I quickly learned early on that talking about competition and teaching the students how to win and how to lose is just as important as the activity itself. I inevitably have had tears in my classroom with yelling and upset students. I have also had students cheer for one another and congratulate each other on the success that was achieved. That is a reality that can occur when students are passionate about competition. But I do not let it end there. We work through the feelings and help everyone to understand the purpose of the game and the competition. The students need to learn how to win graciously and to lose graciously. That is a life skill.

Another factor these experts and probably many teachers overlook is that competition is actually a talent which many students possess and need to develop to reach the fullest potential. These types of students may never be able to discover how good they are without a competition. One of my top strengths is competition. I can remember back to high school, which was longer ago than I would like to admit, I was easily bored in school and at times got into trouble because of the boredom.

In the classroom, my goal was to score the highest grade and also be the first person to finish the test. I also scored exceptionally high on most standardized tests, because I saw it as a competition, but in the classroom, well it was a different story. Most classes were boring, disengaging and seemed to be disconnected from the real world. So, I can relate to students who feel that way, even the ones who perform well. My competitive strength was not developed. But imagine if it had been developed early in life, who knows what I might have achieved.

Did you know?

For female athletes, playing high school sports increases their odds by 41 percent for graduating college compared to non-athletes. http://news.byu.edu/archive07-Jul-GirlsSports.aspx

Ideas to Try

- **Use technology to increase competition**: There are many software programs such as GoNoodle which allow for competitive activities. With this program, you can have competitions within the classroom or have competitions with other classes too. It allows for moderate to vigorous activities like running, which can be done in the classroom. Students simply stand by their desks and can perform activities such as running in place, hurdling in place, stretching, and other exercises along with the GoNoodle videos, which even include Olympic athletes from their respective events.

- **Trash basketball**: This activity is one of those games that can be used as a review before an exam. First the teacher randomly chooses a scorekeeper (using a number between one and one hundred that the students have written down). Then the teacher divides the students into two teams. Questions are asked alternately to members of each team. The teacher asks the questions in order by going down rows of each team. If the student answers the question correctly, she has the choice of taking one point, or she can risk that point and shoot a whiffle ball into the trashcan for three points. If the student misses the shot, then no point is given. However, if the student misses the question, then anyone on the other team can raise his hand to answer the question. The teacher only gives the other team one chance to answer the question, so the team must be certain of the answer. If someone on the other team "steals" a question, then he has the choice of taking a point or shooting for three points as well. The winning team typically gets five points extra credit on their test. Interestingly, some students will study for the trash basketball review game that would not normally study for an exam because they will get to "shoot" if they correctly answer the questions. This is a competition in which every student has the ability to be successful. Because it is a review game, everyone can study and do well, and everyone can get the chance to shoot a ball. Because it is not a typical activity, no one is very good at it, so even non-athletic students tend to have as good an opportunity as the athletic students, which means there is less pressure to make it. So more students try it!

- **Team review with (whiteboard) apps**: Students are put into teams of three or four and each team or student is given a 12x12 whiteboard, dry erase marker, and rag. In this wonderful new age of iPads, we actually use a whiteboard app instead of the boards, marker, and rag. The teacher asks a review question. It really can be any type of question as long as a student can write down the answer on the board. Each student writes the answer and puts it in the middle of the table for the rest of the group to look at. They all nod if they agree with everyone's answers. If they don't agree then the person who doesn't agree writes the answer below the original answer. There is NO TALKING during this review game. Once the group agrees then the boards are turned over. The teacher can set a time limit for each question depending on the question that is being asked. When time is called, the students all hold up the answer that has been written on the iPad. The teacher scans the iPads being held up and gives points to groups that have correct answers. A vital part of the review is everyone hearing the correct answer, which is stated while going over each iPad. At this time students can ask questions. This is both an individual and group review. Every student has time for an individual answer, but then has to work with a team to come up with their team answer. That skill alone is very valuable in working cooperatively with others. This process continues throughout the class. If groups talk or shout out answers then they are not allowed to receive a point, but still need to answer the question. At the end the team that wins gets to pick out of a treat box for a small piece of candy or whatever trinket is in the box. I have played this review game with students ranging from ages 8–16 and every time it is a class favorite. They ask for it before each test.

- **Make it also a personal competition**: This allows students to compete with themselves and to reach personal goals. In our Reading program we use Renaissance Learning and the Accelerated Reading program to enhance reading skills. A new aspect of this program, besides the vocabulary and literacy skills, is the personal reading goals. Students receive a personal goal based on a formula that allows them to compete not only with themselves, but also with classmates to reach the goals. The students have a set period of time to reach their own goal while also being aware of others that reach their own personal goals.

- **Vocabulary relay**: During this activity the class is divided into teams. This can work with as many teams as the teacher can create. The ideal number of students per team is four. Each team will also need a place to write on the board. In my class I usually have four teams of four students with the front whiteboard sectioned off into four parts, one for each team. Each team is given a stack of vocabulary cards with only the definitions on them. A key aspect to this is to number each card. I usually use different colored cards for each team and write the number on one side with the definition on the other. This keeps the sets separate and allows for the terms to be randomly written and one team cannot look to another for the answer. I also have an answer key already generated for each team's set of cards. To play the game the first person reads the definition and then runs to the board to write the term. The student runs back and passes on the deck. The next person reads the next definition and runs to the board to write the answer. This continues until all of the terms have been written. The team to finish first gets 4 bonus points, second 3, third, 2 and last 1 bonus point. Then we all sit down and go over the answers. Two points are given for every correct answer and 1 point is deducted for an incorrect answer. Then the bonus points are added in. The students hang on every answer to learn the point total. This really helps reviewing because the students are really paying attention!

Key Points to Remember

Consider these points when including competition in the classroom:

- The learning and/or growth goal is clearly characterized as valuable.
- The competition has a short duration and is characterized by high energy where all individuals or groups see/have a reasonable chance of winning.
- Focus on short-term competitions between groups such as trivia contests.
- Give opportunities for competition several times throughout the year so students can all experience both success and failure.
- Be sure to talk about the feelings of success and failure and help the students to learn from the experience. They can even make goals to do better next time.
- Boys who are active and engaged in competition will be less likely to become bored or disruptive in the classroom.
- Some students need an environment where they can measure their achievements in a competitive manner to reach their full potential.
- Make competition a positive experience regardless of outcome.
- Incorporate technology for competition, students will immediately connect with this method, such as GoNoodle.

3 | Help Boys Become Readers

" The more that you read, the more things you will know. The more that you learn, the more places you'll go."

Dr. Seuss

Our Thoughts and Some Research Too

Reading is one of the most important skills for a student to develop. For an individual to have any chance at success, he needs to be able to read at a literate level. In fact there are many studies which show a correlation between reading ability and the likelihood students will drop out of high school or the likelihood they will be incarcerated. For instance students who struggle with reading by third grade are four times more likely to drop out of high school. Research by Northeastern University suggests that high school drop outs are 63 times more likely to be incarcerated than high school graduates. If we can improve reading levels of students, then we by default positively affect graduation and incarceration rates. However, no one has stopped to examine what the real issues can be with reading when it comes to male versus female students.

For instance, is reading taught as a skill with real-world value, or has it been reduced to fitting it in for standardized testing? Multiple studies, including a Harvard review on literacy concluded, if students encounter uninspired reading instruction (the famous 'kill and drill' approach) in which they receive no exposure to the many forms and functions of literacy (from making shopping lists to writing one's memoirs) they are unlikely to maintain either the motivation or the purpose to persist.

This is especially true of male readers who are typically behind their female counterparts in reading proficiency. Part of this gap may be attributed to the fact that males aren't typically interested in the same types of books that interest females. Look at the books that men read and you will see a difference between what they find of interest versus women. Men tend to read non-fiction books that are more factual and informational in nature. For instance, some of the bestselling books are focused on leadership, whether it is Steve Jobs (former Apple CEO) or someone like Bobby Bowden (former FSU head football coach). Men also like books about sports, adventure, science fiction, humor, war, and action. There is a reason books like *Sh*t my Dad Says*, and *Not Taco Bell Material* are bestselling books.

It's not that boys or men don't read; it's that they want to read things they enjoy, which, unfortunately, is not always what is chosen for classroom use. If you were to ask a male student about his favorite baseball team, he could probably tell you the batting average of each player and the stats for every pitcher. I remember my nephews could tell me every Dragon Ball Z character, which included names like Goku, Kame-Sen'nin, Yamcha, Tenshinhan, Gohan, and even Yajirobe. They could tell me how to pronounce their name and everything about them. Why? Because it was something in which they were interested.

Boys do like some types of fiction such as sci-fi, fantasy, or humorous books that may be silly or even gross. I (Brad) remember proctoring the CRCT (Criterion Referenced Competency Test) for a group of students a couple of years ago. One male student had finished a section early and he was allowed to read a book. He started giggling while he was reading *Diary of a Wimpy Kid*. I walked back to him and whispered that he had to be quiet because other students were still working. He said he couldn't help it and then he quickly flipped to the back cover where one of the reviews stated, "This book is so hilarious that you will laugh out loud." I almost laughed out loud myself because of his quick wit to show me that it was ok for him to laugh. This is the type of book that many boys would read because it is silly and they can relate to the content.

However, research is clear that boys are lagging behind girls in most areas of reading. Why is there such a gap? Remember that most teachers, especially at elementary level, are female. Female teachers often, even if unconsciously, choose books that are more attractive to girls. These are typically fictional books. When I taught sixth grade science I remember searching for a novel to read in class that was geared towards boys and it was a challenge. There were just not as many options available, which supports the idea that books for classroom use are written more for girls than boys. So what can be done to engage boys in reading? Here are a few factors that influence their reading.

- Boys claim reading becomes less enjoyable as they become older.

- Many adolescent boys fail to see real life applications in what they read. Literature read in Language Arts classes tells "stories" rather than providing useful information. Some boys stop reading because they think there is no practical value in reading.

- As they reach adolescence, more and more boys stop considering themselves readers. Research on the reading attitudes of middle school boys shows that many consider themselves "non-readers."

- Reading is sometimes stereotyped as a "feminine" activity. When boys reach adolescence their gender identification becomes more important. If they believe reading is not a masculine activity, they will abandon it in order to demonstrate their masculinity.

These factors show that boys need to find relevance and a connection to the content that they are reading. Boys are more likely to become engaged in their learning when they feel like it has some application to their lives. They want to read books that pertain to their interests. They also need to see that reading is not a feminine activity, but rather is critical for their personal growth. Boys tend to enjoy reading as it pertains to science and math because it is more informational in nature. Scholastic Books actually have a section on their website called Books for Boys: Reluctant Readers.

While boys generally perform lower than girls on reading assessments, boys do tend to score higher on test questions using informational texts (math and science). Since science and math are written in more of an informational style rather than a narrative style, this may be one of the reasons why boys tend to do better in math or science. Therefore, including more informational type reading in the classroom will also be beneficial to females as well.

So, by choosing more non-fiction or informational books for class reading, boys will be more engaged in reading. Since females tend to score lower in these areas, choosing these informational type of books would potentially improve females' test scores in math and science. While math and science scores have been a concern for females, there has been little focus on incorporating more informational reading for them. Information, or non-fiction books, fit well within the science and the social studies curricular areas.

Reading is critical for improved learning in all content areas. However, for males and females to improve in all areas there has to be attention paid to the types of books read and also to reading beyond books. In the information age, technology can make reading more fun and engaging for students. There are many software programs that include games to help with reading comprehension skills. The key is to offer variety and let students read in areas of interest, so that they find relevance and success. Remember, reading is not just for the classroom, but it is important throughout life. Whether it is for professional development, entertainment, or to learn a new hobby, everyone should enjoy reading at every stage of life.

Reading is a critical aspect to success in the business world. The world is constantly changing and in order to survive, one must always be reading about the changes. While this may seem like a simple concept, it is a main factor that entrepreneurs focus upon. Reading equates with being informed. Being informed means that decisions can be made that will allow businesses to grow and succeed. The reading material often consists of magazine articles, newspaper articles, books, blog posts, and other internet media sources. Successful business owners and entrepreneurs read daily. Note that the type of text they usually read is non-fiction, which shows the importance of incorporating as much non-fiction into the classrooms as possible.

Did you know?

Reading can be therapeutic. People who read are more likely to vote, exercise, and be more cultural. http://www.unbelievable-facts.com/2013/09/10-scientific-facts-about-reading-books.html

Personal Experiences and Stories

When my son was in elementary school his teacher wanted him to read advanced books because a standardized test showed he had a high reading level. The books she "required" were of no interest to him. He stopped reading. It is safe to say he even got to the point of hating reading. I (Julie) met with the teacher and asked her to let him read books of his choice because I cared more about his love for reading. I asked her to add other options, even if they were below his ZPD (zone of proximal development).

She promptly told me that the ZPD is where he needed to be reading. That was when I realized my son, to her, was a test score, not a child. I then went on to explain that I was also an educator and knew exactly what ZPD meant because I happened to have a Masters in Reading and I was a reading diagnostician.

Becoming defensive, she asked me to leave and told me the conference was over. She said I obviously knew more about the subject than her, so it was time that I left. I did not get up and leave. I leaned forward across that table and told her that the conference was not about my level of education; it was about my child and his love for reading. I did not leave. I asked her again to add other options that were more boy-friendly to her list. She was reluctant, but did. Needless to say the relationship between her and my son was strained from then on. My son equates that teacher with the year he hated to read. Teachers have more power than they often realize. By looking beyond the test scores and looking at the individual child, they can work wonders. They may even be able to get a boy to love reading.

I (Julie) have always been a huge fan of reading across the curriculum. When I was hired for my first teaching job 21 years ago I told my principal I was going to use literature in my science class and that is just what I did. I have done it ever since. Sometimes I read non-fiction, sometimes I choose a novel, and sometimes it is just short passages about whatever topics apply. One of my ultimate favorite books to read to my 10-year-olds in science class is *Grossology*. This is probably the book that the boys in my class love the most. Every year I have several who go to Barnes and Noble and purchase their own copies. The book tells about the gross things that happen in the body in a fun and scientific way. I read about barf, diarrhea, blood, belching, and more. This is a perfect complement to my cells to systems unit where we study the major systems within the body. The students beg for me to read every day, and of course, I oblige!

Did you know?

Students who are not on grade level reading by third grade are four–six times more likely to drop out of high school. http://www.aecf.org/~/media/Pubs/Topics/Education/Other/DoubleJeopardyHowThirdGradeReadingSkillsandPovery/DoubleJeopardyReport040511FINAL.pdf

Ideas to Try

- Be sure to have **a mixture of reading material** available in your classroom. Students shouldn't have to miss reading time to go and check out a book. Plan ahead if this is the case and make sure students are prepared for the reading time.

- **As interests change so will reading material**, so be flexible and open-minded when it comes to changing types of reading material available.

- **Give students time to read**: While we tend to have more and more to responsibilities in regards to curriculum and standardized test preparation, it is essential that students are given class time to read. Ideally this should be 20–30 minutes per day!

- **Read when students read**: This modeling of reading makes an impact on students. They often think it is more important if the teacher also takes time to read.

- **Allow for personal choice as well as class reading assignments**: Be sure to give students a choice (within reason) about what they want to read.

- **Recognize learning styles**: Students should have the option to read, listen to, or be read to. They all learn differently. Remember the important aspect is that they are engaging with print. Plan for this! Have headsets available for your students if they want to listen to a book.

- **Be technology tolerant**: iPads, Kindle apps, and Nooks are all vocabulary terms that did not exist when we were younger. Be tolerant to how the students want to read. Again, it is about the reading, not the tool used to read.

- **Use non-fiction within curriculum content**: When teaching science or social studies use informational text within the content that is being studied. For example, if you are teaching science and Newton's Laws, then read parts from a non-fiction text about Newton. If teachers model the use of non-fiction text then students will feel more comfortable reading the texts outside the classroom. Boys will also see that it is relevant to learning.

- **Design novel units around books**: This will enhance the interest in the book while tying the book into other content areas. Students love when they go from one class to another and there are connections. Last year when our students were reading the novel *Abel's Island* in Reading class I designed science activities to expand their reading experience. Students had to design, create, and test devices that Abel could use to survive or get off the island. Every day for a week when the students came in class they would be given a survival scenario that would connect with the part of the book they were reading. This helped the students to be more involved in the reading and also helped them explore the scientific method.

* **Include reading applications**: Boys tend to read the Kid Discover informational reading apps, where girls will read the narrative interactive stories. The boys will also go on the programing/coding apps (such as Hopscotch, Tynker or Code Academy) that teach them basic programing/coding skills. These apps/programs require them to problem solve and strategize. Whereas the girls prefer to write their own creative narrative stories using apps such as Scribble Press, Write About This or Book Creator. Kidblog is another popular writing site and app we use to enhance language art skills. Students will respond to a given prompt or create a free write. They also have the opportunity to not only read each other's writing but comment and collaborate with their peers; a skill they will continue to develop throughout the rest of their lives.

Key Points to Remember

* Remember most boys prefer to read non-fiction. Since science, social studies, and math are written in more of an informational style rather than a narrative style, include them in reading and Language Arts. This exposure will be beneficial to females for science and math as well.

* Let them read in areas of interest (sports, outdoors, adventure, comics), which can include magazines that are suitable for school. They are chunked (shorter texts) and informative.

* Boys are more likely to discuss reading assignments if they are of interest to them.

* Boys need ENCOURAGEMENT with reading.

* Incorporate multimedia in reading.

* Provide opportunities to immediately apply what they have read.

* Provide a variety of assessments, such as book talks.

* Make effective use of targets and challenges.

* Have men as guest readers or authors talk to the class or the whole school.

Inspire Creativity

"It is the supreme art of the teacher to awaken joy in creative expression and knowledge."

Albert Einstein

Our Thoughts and Some Research Too

In a Ted Talks speech a couple of years ago, Ken Robinson discussed how we have killed creativity in the classroom. His point was that schools have abandoned activities/classes such as drama, dance, and other arts. Unfortunately, schools focus on standards and even more so on standardized testing, so anything that doesn't focus directly on testing is being eliminated. Testing, budget cuts, and implementing new curriculum standards have caused many districts to disband their bands, bench their physical education opportunities, erase their drawing courses, and even silence their chorus classes. What Dr. Robinson failed to recognize is that formal education is not the only outlet by which students can increase creativity and the arts are not the method for developing creativity within schools.

Fortunately, there are many outlets for creativity within formal education. As we often suggest, teaching is as much an art as it is a science. Effective teachers cannot only present creative lessons, but provide opportunities for students to be creative as well, to think outside the box, which has become more of a platitude in today's culture rather than a call for true creativity and innovation.

Some may ask why we need to worry about creativity in the classroom. Think of the influence of people like Ludwig van Beethoven, Pablo Picasso, and Jane Austen who created beautiful art, music, and novels which have impacted the world for generations. What if their creativity had been muted? The world would have missed out on their masterpieces. The term creativity is derived from the word create. Isn't education more than memorizing and testing? Shouldn't it be about learning to apply, analyze, and even create? Creativity is really about creating; creating better communication, innovation, expression, and even conceptualization.

Creativity and innovation are the backbones of the entrepreneurial spirit of our country. Inventions, arts, small businesses, and most of what makes America great, have been built by creativity and innovation. Why is creativity and innovation so important for students? Because many of the jobs that we are preparing them for don't even exist today. When we attended school in the 1980s, we had no idea that the internet would drive such a large part of business and the economy in the 1990s and beyond. Who knows what careers and jobs will be created or need to be created in the next 20 years?

Interestingly, research in creativity led to the development of what are now known as gifted or accelerated programs. These programs evolved from the research of Dr. Paul Torrance at the University of Georgia, who was referred to as the father of creativity. Dr. Torrance believed that creativity is a universal potential to be nurtured and enhanced. If creativity is a major component of accelerated or gifted programs, shouldn't it be important for all students? There has to be some recognition by the government to validate that creativity is essential since millions of dollars are being spent in thousands of schools districts all over the United States to build creative arts magnet schools.

In the 1950s advertising executive and educator Alex Osborn, who coined the term brainstorming, started the Creativity Education Foundation. Imagine the creative thought process of someone who was both an educator and advertising executive. In a nutshell, he developed the process known as creativity problem solving. This is the process where ideas are generated through brainstorming, thinking outside the box, connecting, and risk taking. This process leads to creating innovative solutions. The best solutions are identified and then implemented. While this process may not be applicable for every lesson, there are certainly situations where this creative process can benefit a lesson or concept in a variety of subject areas.

Teaching creativity doesn't have to take away from teaching curriculum standards, but rather it reinforces them. Learning to think creatively requires a foundation of knowledge. The creativity aspect, whether it is looking at a topic from a different perspective or finding a different solution, only deepens the understanding of the content. While creativity is a higher order level of thinking (creating), it can also be fun and enjoyable to students. And if we can connect creativity to math and science, how many more students may suddenly enjoy math and science?

Creativity can be included within group projects where collaboration may produce creative ideas or products. But individual work can include creativity as well. In this technological age, it is ok to close the computer and use colored pencils, markers, and actual poster board. Creativity doesn't always have to look neat and uniform like a PowerPoint. Creativity is sometimes drawing outside the lines and getting messy and even noisy!

Think about the topics that are hard to teach and try adding some aspect of creativity to them. One area in which creativity can be utilized is in the area of grammar. Reinforcing grammar is particularly important because students need to be able to speak and write grammatically correct to compete in a global economy, while much of their current communication is informal through social media. One example I have used in the past is to show students the resumes of individuals who didn't get a job because their resumes were filled with grammatical errors. This shows them a real-world situation where proper grammar is important. We also use songs to help learn parts of speech and vocabulary. There are many strategies that can be used to make grammar and language arts more creative and engaging for the students. For example, let your students become characters from a short story or book. Allow them to write to other characters in the story giving them advice. You can let students present a book they have read in a manner in which they choose. For instance, instead of the same old book reports, allow them to make a storyboard, collage, shadow box, or maybe they want to act out part of the story.

Making creativity part of the classroom may mean that teachers step outside their comfort zone, too. Often we teach the way we were taught, which unfortunately tends to be by lecture. Teachers need to give up the control of the class and find ways to be creative themselves. Have you ever had a teacher who dressed up, sang, or acted outside their normal character? Have they found ways to introduce material in a creative way?

Classrooms should exude creativity! Students' works should be proudly displayed as well as pictures taken that document the effort. Students love to see their own work published on the wall or pictures that bring back a meaningful activity. Because of teachers having a creative environment, the students will feel more comfortable exploring with their own creativity.

> **Did you know?**
>
> Creativity builds confidence in students. http://www.creativeconfidence.com/tools

Personal Experiences and Stories

Discussions within a lesson can lead to creative discussion and thinking outside the box. Creativity at its core really is about divergent (multiple solutions) thinking, not simply "the arts." I (Brad) am reminded of the story of a student who was asked to answer the question, "How could you measure the height of a tall building using a barometer?" He was expected to explain that the barometric pressures at the top and the bottom of the building are different, and by calculating, he could determine the building's height. Instead, he answered, "I would tie the barometer to a string, go to the roof of the building, lower it to the ground and then measure the length of the string." His instructor admitted that the answer was technically correct, but did not demonstrate a knowledge of physics. The student then rattled off a whole series of answers involving physics but not one using the principle in question: He would drop the barometer and time its fall. He would make a pendulum and time its frequency at the top and the bottom of the building. He would walk down the stairs marking "barometer units" on the wall. When the instructor finally asked, "what is the 'simplest' answer to the question," the student replied, "I would go to the building superintendent and offer him a brand-new barometer if he will tell me the height of the building!"

When asked if he knew the method that had been suggested for the question, he said "yes, but I am tired of teachers and professors telling me what to think." While this is an extreme example, and the scientist in me even cringes a little, it does ring with a bit of truth and exemplifies divergent thinking. Do we help students learn to think critically (creatively) or simply fill them with information to regurgitate on an exam?

Creativity has become an integral part of my teaching philosophy for two main reasons: I (Julie) enjoy teaching using creativity and my students see growth and experience success because of creativity. Thinking outside the box is a norm in my science class. If the students find one answer, they often have to find another that will also work. My students quickly learn that there are multiple ways to find an answer and solve a problem.

There are two specific projects that my students go back to in their free time after we have done the lessons in class. One is Lego building where they have to modify and change a design to solve a problem. They will spend hours and hours on this! The students have Lego kits where they can build up to nine different designs. We use these regularly in science class. The students will build the design and then they come up with a problem to solve and then redesign the original build. The second is the iPad app Hopscotch. Coding is a concept that I knew nothing about when I was in school, and I am always amazed how the minds of our youth work. This app is basic drag and drop coding where students can create anything! We use the program in science and in math for various activities, but the students take it far beyond that. I have students who have created cities and written their names with numerous codes working simultaneously. This is creativity at its finest!

My son also had an experience that enhanced his confidence in ways that I never thought would occur. At Porter-Gaud, our school, students are encouraged to step outside their comfort zones and try new things. In the Lower School all students have the opportunity to perform on stage for five consecutive years. The middle and upper grades continue to have opportunities for students to grow as artists, actors, and musicians. Our Fine Arts programs are stellar! Needless to say, my child stopped performing after that fifth year and focused entirely on academics. He was not an artist, an actor, nor a musician. He did not think he had a creative bone in his body. That was until he took Studio Art when he was 15. He was encouraged to paint pictures and do various projects. His teacher was amazing. She recognized each student's individual ability and helped him/her grow. I will never forget the day when my son came home and said words that I never thought I would hear, "I am entering an art show." And he did. He didn't win, but that didn't matter. He had confidence that I never saw before in him. That picture is now hanging proudly in our house, and he tells anyone who comes over about how he painted it and actually is a little bit creative!

Did you know?

Stifling creativity is preventing future problem solvers and innovation. http://www.wired.com/2013/10/is-stifling-creativity-in-the-classroom-preventing-future-problem-solvers

Ideas to Try

- **Become technologically savvy!** This means any technology: computers, laptops, iPads, iPhones, tablets, SMART Boards, SMART tables, robotics, YouTube, etc. Be able to blog, tweet, chat, post, code, and more. Once you are comfortable then you will be able to communicate in the world of our students. They are already comfortable there! Bringing any aspect of this in your class will help the students use their creativity.

- **iPads and the apps**: We love Notability, Pages, Numbers, Keynote, iMovie, Prezi, Educreations, and then we have about 100 more on our list that we use off and on throughout the year. Make your own list, but keep it fluid. Be on the look out for new apps. My best resource is my students! They have a form to fill out for new apps they want me to review. Once I review the app then we decide if and how it can be used in class. Last week I had a student tell me that NovaElements was a great way to study the periodic table. Within two days we all downloaded it and explored and built hundreds of elements and compounds. We learned about the periodic table in an innovative way!

- **Creativity is learning**: Create a classroom that recognizes creativity. You may want to design awards or bulletin boards to showcase different ways of solving a problem, or creative solutions to a real-world scenario. Our Humanities and Language Arts classes have publishing stations for students to showcase final pieces of work. Our hallways are lined with material that allows us to hang students' works to be showcased. Our classrooms are decorated with inviting, colorful content that encourages students to want to learn in a fun and imaginative way.

- **Understand that creativity is important to students' future in a global market**: We are preparing for many jobs which don't even exist yet, so they need a skill set which allows them to be creative and innovative in a changing world. Share stories that show this progression with the students. I often tell the students that my parents had the first microwave that was designed or that I remember life without cell phones and the internet. We talk about change and how people were able to capitalize on that change.

- **Encourage curiosity**: Consider what is important to students. Student interests are a great place to start on what drives their own thinking. Find inspiration from their world. Creativity is intrinsic in nature. Try to step into their viewpoint to find what motivates them. Find ways to encourage their own curiosity in and out of the classroom.

- **Include divergent thinking into your discussions or lessons**: Standardized tests do a great job of measuring convergent thinking that includes analytical thinking or logical answers with one correct response. Divergent thinking considers how a learner can use different ways to approach a problem. Remember the example of the barometer? It requires using association and multiplicity of thought.

- **Think of creativity as a skill**: Much like resourcefulness and inventiveness, it is less a trait and more a proficiency that can be taught. If we see it this way, our job as educators becomes to find ways to encourage its use and break it down into smaller skill sets.

- **Let them lead**: Often when teachers assign a project, they give a rubric for the students to follow which stifles the creativity. So occasionally, allow students to develop their own rubrics for a project. Allow students to collaborate on projects, problem solving, or even homework. Give the students a chance to be vested in their own education. You will be amazed at what they can accomplish!

- **Find community support**: Many organizations work to support the arts in schools. Look for ones in your area that can help supplement your existing curriculum. You may be surprised by what you can achieve. These may be especially useful in schools where the arts have been cut because of budget deficits.

- **Failure is not fatal**: Effective teachers create safe environments where students can take risks without fear of being wrong or failure. Failure is part of learning and growth. It also gives the students an opportunity to reassess, make adjustments, and find better solutions. Reflection is an excellent way to help grow from failure.

- **Don't praise neatness**: Let students explore, imagine, generate, and create. Conforming to a set of standards brings us back to the assembly-line model. Structure and set guidelines are fine; students should have some boundaries.

- **Include student choice**: When students feel that they have the power to choose how to represent their understanding of content it allows their creativity and unique style to shine through. Students are empowered when their creations are shared with other students, parents or community members. Some of the apps that students choose from to represent the concepts they have learned are as follows: Book Creator, Educreation, Write About This, and Pic Collage.

Key Points to Remember

- Create a safe environment where students aren't afraid to take risks, such as create their own projects or presenting information in a creative manner.

- Think of creativity as a skill that students will need to succeed in the real world. Creativity and innovation are qualities of successful entrepreneurs.

- Use students' interests to engage them in the classroom and pique their curiosity and creativity.

- Embrace creativity as part of teaching and learning.

- Model creativity in your teaching.

- Incorporate divergent thinking when appropriate. Divergent thinking considers how a learner can use different ways to approach a problem.

- Creativity can be messy and loud, which can be fun for the students.

- We are educating children for jobs that may not even exist yet, so they need creative and innovative skills to be able to succeed.

Here is a creative way to learn all of the info above! (My kids love Wordle!)

Encourage Meaningful Engagement

"Give the pupils something to do, not something to learn; and the doing is of such a nature as to demand thinking; learning naturally results."

John Dewey

Our Thoughts and Some Research Too

Most of us understand that lecturing from a textbook is not the best method for student engagement in the classroom. However, we may rush to do activities because we think they are engaging the students. But are these activities used simply for the sake of saying we aren't lecturing? Students want to do activities that have a purpose and are not simply time fillers. We have to be able to generate activities that will allow students to experience being meaningfully engaged with content. If they can experience it in schools then they will be able to transfer that to the real world when they are in their professions.

What does being engaged with content mean? According to Newt Barrett, the President of Voyager Media, "Genuinely engaging content is so attractive and appealing that it **disarms you from your very first encounter . . . and makes you want to linger to learn more.** When it really connects with you, it will take your breath away. It's **a little bit like love at first sight**" (http://contentmarketinginstitute.com/2010/09/what-does-engaging-content-mean). Content that is engaging offers a new way to look at material, and stirs up feelings of interest and even excitement. It can also give you the feeling that there is even more to look forward to. Can you imagine teaching content where this is the case? Can you imagine your students falling in love or becoming emotionally attached to content because of how they were able to engage with it in your classroom? Can you imagine the students having that feeling so much in our classrooms that they would crave it when they went out into the real world?

Consider the analogy of two people swimming in a race. The first swimmer dives in and quickly swims the length of the pool. The other swimmer dives in but begins to tread water rather than swim to the other end. The swimmer treading water is working very hard to stay afloat; in fact he is working as hard as the other swimmer. But, are both swimmers making the same amount of progress? If you answered "No" then you are correct! The one treading water is working hard, but not making any progress, but simply staying afloat. Now, as a teacher, are you incorporating activities that simply keep the students busy (afloat) or are you using activities that actually help the students reach an end goal where they experience progress? Students need to know the difference between just working hard and working hard to reach the end goal with a sense of achievement and obtaining something new. It is knowing how to recognize and reach that end goal that will help them pursue a career which they are passionate about and not make them satisfied just going through the motions to earn a paycheck.

Have you ever seen a baseball team that simply discussed playing the sport? No, they practice and engage in the activity. The coach is constantly teaching them new plays and challenging their thinking. There are people who love baseball. That is directly correlated with the opportunity they had to be engaged with the sport. What about an orchestra? Do they come to rehearsal and simply read the music or watch a video of a concert? No, they actually play their instruments. Again, they have a love for music. It touches them on a level that other things do not. Engaged learning in the classroom is no different. Will a student learn more if you show him a picture of a dissected frog, or if he actually dissects the frog himself?

Think about students today compared to students of 20 years ago. Today's culture requires us to relate to the students' world before we can think about engaging them. They have unlimited access to information, so we have to provide more than just data dumping. In fact, relevant, meaningful activities that both engage students emotionally and connect with what they already know help build neural connections and long-term memory storage.

Neurologist Judy Willis suggests that the brain processes underlying this may involve the reticular activating system, or RAS, the brain's first filter for incoming sensory information (sights, sounds, and so on). It acts like a virtual editor of sensory information, letting in certain things and filtering out others. Information has to make it through the RAS to get to parts of the brain where it can be "acknowledged, recognized, coded into patterns, and ultimately stored in long-term memory." What tends to get through? Willis explains that the RAS prioritizes potential threats and things that are new, pique curiosity, or have the potential to bring pleasure.

This means traditional methods of random facts and impersonal delivery of content will have difficulty infiltrating the students' brains. Especially when you consider children today are exposed to more information by the age of 5 than their grandparents were by the age of 18. This means children are exposed to sensory overload. So, the content has to be meaningful and relevant to the students. In fact, students who receive meaningful instruction are more likely to show an understanding of advanced skills by the end of the school year. Keep in mind that by making instruction meaningful the students are recognizing what is relevant. They will continue to crave that relevant feeling as they go through life.

Activities require a focus on relevance and meaning, not just busy work. If it is only about disseminating information for a standardized test, then students could simply connect to the Wi-Fi at McDonald's and Google information all day. We need to make sure we are helping the students engage with the content at all times. The engagement with the content is going to help the students make connections, which will deepen the understanding. Students will then be able to recognize what it means to delve deeper into subject area content. Continued exposure to this type of connection will not only enhance the level of learning, but it will help the students to recognize and desire this type of interaction with new content as it is covered. When students start to look outside of the classroom and go into the job market, they will continue to crave this meaningful engagement. Hopefully students will know what it is like to want to know more about a topic and not just settle for status quo. Those students will be prepared to be entrepreneurs, inventors, and designers. They will be able to take a concept given to them and reach new and exciting levels. These students will be given the tools through experience to thrive in the real world.

The teacher/student engagement is critical to content being passed on from one person to another. A major concern is when new teachers can't relate to the different learning styles and interests in the classroom. Why? Because the teachers were typically female and good students themselves, who worked hard and never got into trouble. They were often self-motivated and craved the sense of that deepened engagement with the content. That makes sense because many knew they wanted to be teachers so they wanted to interact with the content area that they were already passionate about.

Research shows that girls are more likely to sit quietly for extended periods of time and do worksheets or activities without disruptions while male students may be bored or over-active. This difference in learning style becomes a barrier and teachers must learn how to get past that barrier and engage with all students in the class. It's important to create a learning environment that will connect with all students and not just the ones who are well behaved and hardworking regardless of the delivery method. The teachers also need to recognize that not all of the students are passionate about learning and may not be naturally interested in deepening their understanding. By recognizing different learning styles and interests, the teacher can then successfully generate lessons that enable all students to experience learning at a deeper level of content.

Engaging with the community is another important aspect for students to learn and our schools are a place where that can happen. There are numerous ways that this can occur. If programs are cut due to budgets, bring in guest speakers or programs that will help students enhance the skills that have been removed from the curriculum or school day. This can enhance their level of learning and expose them to new material. Going on a field trip can serve the same purpose. Students can be exposed to material that may not be available in the classroom. Service learning is another aspect that is invaluable. This type of engaging builds character and helps students learn more about what the real world is like. They can volunteer and become engaged with programs in which they are passionate. By being engaged with these programs they will learn more about them and take an interest that will deepen their level of understanding. We are a borderless world with the internet and with the possibilities of travel. Engaging with the community is an aspect that needs to be a part of our education systems.

Did you know?

Encouraging engagement in the workplace helps with retention rate of employees. http://www.forbes.com/sites/sylviavorhausersmith/2013/08/14/how-the-best-places-to-work-are-nailing-employee-engagement

Personal Experiences and Stories

Since our school has adopted iPads, we still do vocabulary terms, but we now interact with every word! The iPads have allowed for personal engagement with each and every vocabulary term we study. How cool is that?! The students have the option of taking pictures that explain or relate with the terms or leaving themselves messages that will make personal connections with the terms. Students who like the notecard method have an app in which they can create their own notecards and study program. Since we have used the iPads, the students' vocabulary comprehension has increased dramatically because they are engaged with the terms. The learning process is personal and meaningful, not just a time-consuming boredom of copying definitions from a glossary. The students are even given time in the year to explore beyond what they learned. This is a couple days set aside to pursue a topic or idea that they want to know more about. Each year I am afraid I will have some student who needs help finding an idea, but in my 21 years of teaching that has never happened. I am amazed how passionate they have become about some of the topics we have covered.

With individual activities you can allow the students to express their own personalities and interests. Have you ever thought about having the students do a book talk rather than a book report? Who better to sell or pitch a book than the students themselves? My son's English class had an independent reading assignment where the culmination was a talk show interview. The students were either the author or the editor of the book. The individual students were obviously engaged because of the level of work that was done before the presentations, but so was the rest of the class because there was audience participation along with the interviews. Numerous students wanted to read books that appealed to them that they learned about during the talk show. This creative way of assessing that students read a book became a hit and has been modeled by other teachers in the school. Another individual activity that my children have experienced is when they became a historical character during a given time period. Think about it; they can describe a historical event or setting and then create their own version of it. These types of individual activities give the students an opportunity to add their personalities to an assignment and create something that is personalized while learning important academic content. This same teacher provided so many engaging activities during the school year that my child actually designed a trip because of his experience.

In our family when a child turns 13 he is able to design the family vacation. So when it came time for that to occur we asked our son where he wanted to go. He did not even hesitate. He said, "Northern France." My husband and I just looked at each other in confusion. My son went on to describe the beaches of Normandy and exuded his passion for history as he began his discourse of why that was where he wanted to go. I immediately thought of his teacher. This came from the classroom and from my child being able to interact with history on a personal level. Needless to say he walked those beaches and toured the museums and gravesites. His passion continues but it is all because it was generated in that sixth grade History class.

My younger child, age 14, flew to Costa Rica with a group of students and teachers this year to work at Kids Save the Rain Forest. This opportunity helped him develop a respect for a different culture by engaging directly with people from that country. He followed a passion to help others and was able to become emotionally invested in a way the classroom could not provide. My older son, age 16, just returned from a trip to Italy where he was able to engage with a different culture with 34 other students, teachers, and administrators. The connection with the content from his Latin class, Religion class, and History classes was invaluable. He was engaging with the content, a different culture, his classmates, and teachers all while in another community in a different country. Again, this type of meaningful engagement with the outside community was something that could not happen within the walls of the school building.

Did you know?

Motivation, engagement and achievement are directly correlated. http://www.ascd.org/publications/books/107034/chapters/Student-Motivation,-Engagement,-and-Achievement.aspx

Ideas to Try

- **Set a goal to minimize lecturing**: There is a time and place for lecture. Just be sure to allow for student engagement with the content at some time during the class period. This may be outside of your comfort zone, so start with an amount you are comfortable with and then increase the amount of engagement until you reach your desired goal.

- **Group projects**: Put students in groups and allow them to work together on a meaningful activity. Be sure to have a clear plan for assessment with group guidelines for behavior expectations. Often students will feel group work is not fair, so be clear about expectations of all group members. The group work should encourage engagement. This can be group work or teamwork. Be sure to be clear if everyone does his or her own thing towards a final goal or if collaboration needs to occur and students must interact with each other to reach an overall goal.

- **Jigsaw and beyond**: Jigsaw is a cooperative learning tool where students are put in groups where each student is sent to a station to master specific content. Then the students all return from their stations to teach their original group members the content in a way that they have learned it. This gives students responsibilities along with personalized learning opportunities. The next step (or the beyond portion) is for the students to take one of the concepts they learned or shared and delve deeper. What part do they want to know more about? What questions have not been answered for them in regards to the content? Give them class time to explore and then share what they learned.

- **Students teach content**: Let students be creative and have responsibility at the same time! This can happen when students teach content to the class. First and foremost, let them choose a topic that they want to explore more and deepen their understanding. For example, in science they conduct science experiments at home and have a 10-minute presentation with a demonstration of a science concept. Remember when doing this the other students have to be able to be engaged, too. If not, then it is just like lecturing with you in front of the room. That is why a time limit and demonstration with the potential for interaction is an important aspect of this idea.

- **Student-generated scavenger hunts**: These are a class favorite because for the students this is engagement with movement! I have the students find a cool fact about what we are studying and create a QR code for it. Then I put QR codes around campus and have the students find the clues and complete the question or activity at each station. Similar activities have been done in foreign language classes and science classes. Students love it! It piques their interest about what others wrote, lets them share their passion, and keeps them involved in obtaining the curricular content.

- **Focus on literary skills**: Students are being asked to delve into deeper learning and understanding. This often means reading beyond their grade level or learning about content that is challenging. By focusing on literary skills the students will be prepared to tackle this challenge.

- **Develop a community service program**: Join or create a program of your own. This will allow students, teachers, and anyone within your school community to engage with others in need in outside communities. You can have a general program where students can volunteer on their own at places of their own choice. You can also have a school program where groups go to help programs that are connected with your school. The best way to do this is to have your students brainstorm service programs in which they are interested in helping. Have those program directors or workers associated with the programs come to your school to share information. Depending on your population, choose an appropriate amount that you can truly help. Create groups and a set schedule of when people will participate in the community service programs. At our school, Porter-Gaud School, we have a Service Learning Director who coordinates service programs for over 900 students in grades 1–12 (ages 6–18). We have school-wide programs such as Philanthropy Week, World Food Day, and Water Missions just to name a few. There are more than 25 different service projects available for students to choose to engage with and become a productive member of society.

- **International travel**: This will give students and teachers the opportunity to engage with other cultures outside their own. Teachers who are interested in starting this type of travel program should look into programs where the trips are already designed. Our school has used ACIS for numerous trips. Programs that are established help with teacher training and already have done lots of the legwork needed to successfully provide the safest and most meaningful trip for your students.

- **Guest speakers and programs**: Bring in people from the community to interact with your school community. This can be in any subject area or sports teams. It can be as a guest speaker or even someone who will come in and help with a program. It can also be a parent who has a connection with the community. One of our teacher's parents is a fire fighter and he brings a truck over for our first graders to see. Our fifth graders make their own river cane flutes during a program when a story teller/musician comes to our school for a week. This helps acknowledge passions that we cannot reach inside the walls of our school.

Key Points to Remember

Remember these ideas for encouraging engagement:

- Meaningful engaging means having a personal connection with the content that allows a deepening of understanding to occur.
- Provide opportunities for students to be able to engage with content through exploration and hands-on projects and activities.
- Let the students have ownership in the learning process and allow them to choose their own topics when suitable.
- Provide support for higher levels of learning by enhancing reading and literacy skills.
- Provide opportunities to engage with the outside community.

6 Help Students Find Their Voices

" One word expresses the pathway to greatness: voice. Those on this path find their voice and inspire others to find theirs. The rest never do. "

Steven Covey

Our Thoughts and Some Research Too

Most people might think education is a place for sharing of ideas, discussing differences of ideas, and a place where every voice can be heard. The "voice" we're referring to is not a physical, audible voice or expression which is belligerent or disrespectful or constant. But, rather it is the ability to voice our views and beliefs in a respectful manner, especially when they differ from others. This is in sharp contrast to the reality of public education where students are rarely giving an opportunity to speak their "voice."

Unfortunately, this thinking has created generations of adults who also don't know how to speak their "voice." Most adults lack the skills to confront negative situations or to speak out when they experience or observe wrong doings. How many times does an administrator or boss speak harshly to someone with no consequence? In some instances, it is not that they don't want to speak up, but they lack the skills to do so effectively.

Anyone can speak their voice when things are going their way or when their point of view matches another's point of view. However, the challenge is to speak one's voice in the face of differing points of view and competing objectives.

Hopefully the content throughout this book will help you empower students with the strengths, passion, and integrity to find their "voice." Students are empowered by teachers, parents, and coaches who sincerely care for them, affirm their work, and encourage them to reach their highest potential. The students are moved and inspired by that kind of relationship. As Dr. Michele Borba, author of *The Big Book of Parenting Solutions*, explains, "Provide opportunities for your child to be a member of a team or lead others. You might enroll your child in public speaking or theater to build confidence in speaking in front of others. Find a platform that fits your child's passions, talents, and comfort level!"

Once students find their voice, they need to be able to communicate their voice in an effective and productive manner. Proper communication is essential to having our "voice" heard. If students respond in an inappropriate manner, then they lose credibility. So it is important to help them learn the correct way to express their ideas and views.

Public speaking is an essential skill to express your thoughts, feelings, and ideas to a large group of people. However, many people are afraid of public speaking, which makes it even more difficult to speak up when you feel like you should be heard. This is why it is so important for students to develop their public speaking skills so they will be able to share their voice and feel comfortable enough to focus on connecting with their audience.

We have a close friend who is also an author and international speaker in education. Her "voice" is similar to ours in that she is dedicated to improving education for teachers and especially students. She once shared a story of having to speak directly after Bill Gates at a major educational conference. She said that even after years of speaking and presenting, she was terrified because she was speaking right after Bill Gates!

However, as his speech progressed, she became less terrified because it was apparent that he wasn't comfortable with public speaking. Here was a brilliant individual as well as one of the richest people in the world, but he just couldn't seem to connect with the audience. She said by the end of his speech, she was actually looking forward to stepping on stage.

Although he founded Microsoft, Gates was not really a public figure and had little public speaking experience when he first began public speaking to enhance his charitable foundation and other charitable endeavors, including education. Gates realized that selling ideas requires more than facts and figures: A presentation must be engaging and connect with the audience in order to get people to take action. So, he consciously worked on his presentation skills and finding his voice, so he could better connect with others on topics he is passionate about.

Even the youngest of students can give speeches to their classmates. The length can vary depending on the topic and the age of the student; the important thing is to give the opportunity. The students have to be given the opportunity to practice this skill in order for the skill to develop. This includes experiencing both failure and success. Reflection after presentations will help to work through times when the students did not experience total success. When students watch one another give speeches or presentations they are not only seeing the skill modeled, but they are also going through the journey with others. There is comfort to that. Students will gain confidence and build their self-esteem the more they practice finding their voice.

There are numerous benefits to public speaking. Public speaking will help develop leadership skills, boost communication skills, improve listening skills, develop more powerful creative thinking skills, organize your thoughts, and inspire others (http://www.self-esteem-health.com/importance-of-public-speaking.html). When connecting the writing component to any presentation the writing and reading skills also improve. These types of skills will open doors of opportunities for students and allow them to follow their calling and excel in life.

Another important aspect of communicating your voice effectively is utilizing empathy. Empathy is the ability to relate to how someone is feeling and respond with care and compassion. It is one of the most important skills that we can exhibit. It will lead to greater success personally and professionally and will allow you to become happier the more you practice having empathy. We consider empathy to be like excellence in that it is not an act, but it is a habit, it is a skill that has to be developed. So help students become aware of how they speak to others and interact with others. Help them focus on being positive and encouraging to others. Help them develop skills to help build others up rather than putting them down. These skills will stay with them and be an asset when they go into the real world.

One of the reasons that empathy is lacking in our culture is that people no longer interact face to face. People are too occupied checking emails, sending texts, or messaging on their phone to interact with people in person. Empathy requires spending time listening and observing the people around you. It requires face-to-face communication.

There are also many benefits to people who are empathetic. Individuals who utilize empathy tend to treat other people better. They will have less trouble dealing with interpersonal conflict personally and professionally. They will be able to more accurately predict the actions and reactions of the people with whom they interact. They will also learn how to motivate the people around them because they will better understand their motivations and fears. These are wonderful attributes to teach our students so they can use them all throughout their lives.

Finally, confrontation is one of the key factors in effectively communicating your voice. Besides public speaking, confrontation is also a fear many people possess. Most people simply aren't comfortable confronting others. It's quite normal to feel uneasy approaching someone to voice a complaint or an unmet need. If, however, you dread confrontation so much that you opt for peace at *any* price, you might be settling for unhappiness.

Confrontations can occur in many forms and in many different aspects of our lives. Students may have to deal with conflict on the playground, with their friends, a bully, parents, or a multitude of other situations. Even as adults, we are not immune to confrontation. We may have issues with a spouse, children, or even our boss.

Confrontation does not mean fight. It means: state what you have to say, even if you are scared or afraid, and then listen to what they have to say. Many times it may actually end right there. Some important points regarding confrontation that will benefit students are:

- Focus on the specific issue, don't bring up other issues or make it about the individual, keep the focus on the specific problem.
- Listen carefully to the other person's responses to your complaint, even restating important points if necessary.
- Don't focus on simply being "right" but focus on relating to the other person and finding a solution.
- Bring up issues – don't avoid them. The confrontations we avoid eventually become the ugly conflicts we can no longer avoid.

Did you know?

As a leader, the importance of public speaking cannot be overemphasized.
http://www.leadership-with-you.com/importance-of-public-speaking.html

Personal Experiences and Stories

Public speaking is a regular part of my (Julie's) science class. Students will be the reporter within the lab groups, which means that they will share information with the class. They also present various projects throughout the year. During the first week of school I tell my students that public speaking is something that everyone will experience throughout the year numerous times and that a goal of mine is for everyone to be comfortable speaking in front of their peers. As I say this several people often look down or tend to squirm a little in their seats. The sense of uneasiness usually pierces through the room.

That is when I share a story. I tell them about a girl who once stood in front of the class to give a speech on the Greek goddess Athena. I describe how this girl chose to lean on a podium instead of stand in plain sight in front of the whole class. I go on to share how her voice cracked a little when she started to speak and how she could barely look up from the paper in front of her. Then I go on to say how as she said her first few words the color of her cheeks went from pink to a ghostly white. I describe how the blood could be seen draining from her face and how then she started to sway. By this time the class is usually dead silent and feeling bad for the girl. They are hanging on to every word. I continue by describing how the girl swayed one time, but instead of swaying back to standing, she continued and fell right to the floor knocking over the podium as she went down. She had passed out in front of the whole class.

At that point I usually hear some gasps and the students sympathize with the girl. Then immediately start asking questions. That is when I let them know that instance did not stop me from learning how to speak in front of people and they are often shocked when they find out that I was that girl. Embarrassing? Yes. But it was a good learning experience and that specific teacher helped me find my voice. Now I can speak in front of pretty much anyone at any time. This story helps the students know that I don't expect perfection when speaking in front of the class and that this will be a journey that we all take together. They know I want to help them find their voice.

One glowing example that I (Brad) use with my students is of an individual whose voice influenced the world: William Wilberforce. He was a wealthy man who was a member of the British Parliament. He was a man who could have simply enjoyed his station in life and his position of power. However, after meeting Thomas Clarkson, his life changed dramatically and he felt his calling was to help end the slave trade and slavery. For 18 years he regularly introduced anti-slavery motions in parliament, but to no avail. Even though he was mocked, threatened, and faced much opposition, he was relentless in his calling to help end slavery.

In 1807, the slave trade was abolished, but this did not free those who were already slaves. Wilberforce did not let this dissuade him from his calling to ensure that all people were free. He continued to fight for the end of slavery until he retired from politics in 1825. Even in retirement, he continued to work tirelessly to abolish slavery. In 1833, after fighting for the abolishment of slavery for nearly 45 years, Wilberforce received word that there were enough votes to finally abolish slavery. Wilberforce died just a few days later, having seen his life's work complete. This one man had used his voice to change the world. I have had several students who have shared that this man's story profoundly affected them, as it has me as well.

Did you know?

According to Confucius, "Choose a job you love, and you will never have to work a day in your life." http://zenhabits.net/the-short-but-powerful-guide-to-finding-your-passion

Ideas to Try

- **Provide opportunities to build confidence**: This can be any activity that will allow students to practice a skill and experience success. The skills include communication, leadership, competition, and team building.

- **Public speaking**: Give students the opportunity to present to the class or a group. Make sure the speeches or presentations are clearly written and practiced in front of fake audiences before the real event. The project or report should already be assessed so that the final presentation is equivalent to the publication stage of a writing piece. Remember to give feedback. If students are shy or introverted, you may let them speak in front of smaller groups until they gain more confidence.

- **Watch public speeches as models**: Let the students attend a speech debate or event. Find a way for the students to see others present a clear, cohesive speech that holds the students' attention. Be sure to show good and bad examples so the students can learn what to do and what not to do.

- **Interview and introductions**: The students must interview and introduce someone to their class. This can be other classmates, but it also can be fictitious. I have had students introduce each other at the beginning of the school year. I have also had students research inventors and then introduce them to the class. This helps students connect with one another and practice public speaking.

- **Practice eye contact, proper posture, and relaxed breathing**: Students may not be comfortable standing in front of the class. I (Julie), myself, have passed out giving speeches. It is important the students know how to stand, how to look around, and to be aware of their breathing. These concepts may seem simple, but they are important to help the audience feel valued and included in the discussion. Knowing these techniques will help students successfully deliver a speech which will help build their confidence.

- **Speech competitions**: Allow your students the opportunity to compete in a speech event. This can be a debate or a contest. Our students participate in the Poetry Out Loud competition yearly. All students grades 6–12 enter the competition by presenting to their class. The winners of the class competition then go on to the school competition. The school winners have the opportunity to compete statewide.

- **Practice syllabication**: Students often stammer over words and then lose the flow of the presentation. Allow students to practice with tongue twisters and phrases that will help them enunciate. (Try saying red leather, yellow leather over and over again. Our speech teacher has all students do this prior to going to the podium.)

- **Conflict resolution**: This is a program where students work through their own disagreements. Students practice listening and working through their problems in a respectful and productive manner. There are specific steps and training that correlates with the program. I became a certified trainer and have worked with students year after year to teach them the techniques. These techniques will hopefully stick with them in the years to come. They will know how to work through conflict while having their voice heard and respected.

- **Discuss empathy** in the classroom. What does it mean? Provide definitions. What images of empathy do you see on TV, in the movies, and so on? Show examples.

- **PUT-UPS (teachablemoment.org)**: Ask, "What is a put-down?" Sometimes people say hurtful things to one another. Such remarks tell a person that he or she is no good, not important, and "less than" other people. That's why they are called "put-downs." Ask for two or three examples of put-downs. Discuss the following:

○ Where do people learn put-downs?

○ How do put-downs make people feel?

○ Why do we say put-downs?

If people in the class say these things to one another, how might it affect the group? Ask the class to think of put-ups, that is, kind and friendly things to say to each other. List the contributions on chart paper. Discuss the following:

○ How would these words make someone feel?

○ What would be the effect on the class if we used these phrases instead of put-downs?

● **Group discussions**: Encourage students to speak up in group discussions. Especially if they have a differing view or opinion. Just like practicing public speaking, the more students practice the more comfortable they will become speaking up in other groups, even if they are nervous or scared.

Key Points to Remember

● Finding one's voice is the ability to voice our views and beliefs in a respectful manner, especially when they differ from others.

● Provide opportunities for students to speak out in class, group discussions, and to speak in front of groups or even the whole school.

● Give students the opportunity to write, perform, watch, and critique speeches and presentations.

● Helping students find their voice will not only help them in school, but will also set them up for success in the real world.

● Guide students through techniques to handle confrontation effectively.

Incorporate Edutainment and Pop Culture

"Learning should be a joy and full of excitement. It is life's greatest adventure."

Taylor Caldwell

Our Thoughts and Some Research Too

Since the times of Socrates, education has been about the teacher imparting knowledge to students. Even as late as the turn of the twenty-first century, most new knowledge or information was transmitted from teacher to student. There was no Internet to provide different platforms for delivering information from around the world. Before the technology explosion, where else would you learn this information except from your teacher? The teacher held "the keys to the informational kingdom" and if you didn't attend school, well then you simply missed out.

However, over the past 20 years, our sources of information have expanded beyond the teacher and beyond the school walls. As we mentioned earlier, a child today is exposed to more information by the age of 5 than her grandparents were by the age of 18. This means students are already exposed to more information before entering school than their grandparents were exposed to by the time they graduated high school. Yet, we think formal education is still the only means by which students acquire knowledge?

If we consider the profound influence of movies, music, video games, and even social media on our students, pop culture is anything but irrelevant. The hesitancy of some educators to embrace pop culture may be because they feel their job is only to teach the content of their subject area or others may simply not feel comfortable utilizing technology or cultural influences in the classroom. Often teachers think there is a disconnect between pop culture and formal education. Yet, research suggests the students are influenced more by pop culture than formal education. So, if students are going to dismiss one as irrelevant, guess which one they will choose?

Part of the problem is that education tries to keep a division between formal learning and the real world. Even Plato believed that students should be trained by what amuses their minds, not by harshness and force. Take for instance technologies like iPods and cell phones. These have been banned in most schools and districts. The reality is that iPods and cell phones are a vital part of everyday life for many students, so why not allow them in the classroom? There are some forward thinking districts that do allow them in schools, but the number is minuscule in comparison to the number of schools that do not. When properly supervised and implemented within the curriculum, these technologies can enhance the learning experience. Students know that professionals (like their parents) employ digital tools such as laptops and mobile devices in their everyday work, yet these are often prohibited from their learning experience. Surely it must be frustrating to students to attend schools intending to prepare them for the business world and yet not be allowed the very tools used in the real world.

Edutainment is the idea of connecting formal learning to the real world in a fun, entertaining, and engaging manner. I (Brad) first used the term several years ago in my book *The Edutainer* and some educators have implemented the term as a buzzword in more recent years. As I stated above, students are influenced more by pop culture than by formal education. This is because most of our instruction is as dated as the Dewey Decimal system. For example, think about how many teachers still give the students long lists of vocabulary words to learn or have to memorize and spell. The lists have no personal relevance and do not resonate with a specific topic about which the student has been engaged. That means the vocabulary terms are likely to be blocked by the brain's affective (or emotional) filters. This means the student's brain actually shuts down instead of learning the words. But again, teachers still give lists week after week.

To reach them, students need a personal connection to the material, whether that's through engaging them emotionally or connecting the new information with previously acquired knowledge (often one and the same). Without that, students may not only disengage and quickly forget, but they may also lose the motivation to even try.

If students appear bored or unengaged, it may simply be the fact that the content is delivered in a manner that is not effective in capturing and maintaining their attention. Remember the students are on sensory overload in the Information Age, so we are competing for their attention in the classroom.

The content has to be delivered by a method that gets the students' attention. It also has to make a connection with the real world for it to have value and meaning. If learning is deemed valuable and important to the student, then the educator doesn't need a scripted curriculum or a fad initiative that has students and the educator jumping through hoops. There shouldn't be weekly spelling and vocabulary lists of random words to be memorized, spit back out, and then discarded.

Edutainment is the philosophy through which we make the learning process relevant and applicable to the "real world" of the twenty-first century. Edutainment bridges the gap between traditional school and the real world. When this gap is bridged, students not only realize the relevance of education but will also take ownership of their learning. Remember you now know your students' interests, so introduce and build lessons around their world and the real world as much as possible. Any subject can be connected to the students' lives. Make the learning fun and entertaining.

In the technology age, schools need to recognize that students are a consumer. While education is compulsory to a certain age, attending your school is not. Students have choices now that simply didn't exist a couple of decades ago. Besides the obvious private schools, there are now magnet schools, charter schools, virtual schools, and even for-profit schools that are entering the formal education scene. With a virtual education, the student doesn't even have to leave her home and can even live in another country. There are students in Saudi Arabia, for example, who are attending virtual schools in the US. All they need is a computer and an Internet connection. So, the days of the assembly-line mentality of schooling where students come to the warehouse, get lost in the crowds and try to survive is no longer relevant. So make school a place they want to attend, because they no longer "have" to attend.

Did you know?

On average, a child laughs 300 times a day while an adult laughs only 17 times a day. Learning needs to be fun and both teachers and students will enjoy the laughter. http://www2.ca.uky.edu/hes/fcs/factshts/hsw-caw-807.pdf

Personal Experiences and Stories

I (Brad) remember attending a professional development workshop several years ago, which was focused on math. The trainer was discussing the age old question that students always ask, "When will I ever use this?" Her reply was to tell students that they will need it one day. My first thought was, "What? You are going to tell a child in class that he won't use the information until *one day*?" When will the child decide he needs to learn it? That's right, One day . . . or sadly, maybe never. Regardless of the math topic, there is a way to connect it to their world. The more relevant students find education in regards to the real world, the more they will value education and therefore be better prepared for the real world.

Another teacher shared that her students complained about doing vocabulary and didn't understand why they needed to define the words. She decided to find some acceptable songs that used many of the vocabulary words. The teacher then had the students divide up into groups and listen to the songs to find the vocabulary words within the songs. When the students could identify them in the lyrics, they had to determine the meaning of the words. Of course, they had to use dictionaries and did learn the meaning of each. The students were engaged and actually enjoyed the activity. Simply put; sometimes you have to think "outside the box" to find solutions that don't fit the plain brown box.

What about putting vocabulary to music and bringing in pop culture in that way? In my fifth grade science class the students had to write and perform a cell rap or song to show they understood each of the terms for the organelles within the plant and animal cell. They were able to choose their own background music and even add dance moves. Not only did the students learn the terms for the activity, I saw numerous students bobbing their heads on the test to a beat within their heads as they answered questions about those organelles. To take it one step further, the sixth grade science teacher often would tell me the students share their songs with her when they study the cell . . . almost eight months later! That's when I know as a teacher that I have done something right with teaching the vocabulary this way!

Can you imagine teaching a whole set of lessons based on a song alone? Try listening to "*We Didn't Start the Fire*" by Billy Joel. Now can you imagine making that the basis of teaching a unit in History class? My son's seventh grade teacher did just that. I am amazed that four years later he not only knows every line to the song, but he understands and can explain every connection to history. Now that is edutainment at its finest!

I (Julie) just returned from a field trip with my fifth grade science students. After studying forces and motion the students went to a local amusement park/miniature golf course and had to complete activities based on what they learned. They calculated the speed of the go-carts, applied Newton's Laws while jumping in the Jump Castle and sliding down the giant slide. They also completed various challenges and activities while playing 18 holes of miniature golf. To make a math connection our math teacher designed a collaborative activity where the students identified and applied geometry concepts while playing the second miniature golf course. I am almost embarrassed to admit that I happened to be using the facilities when two of our parent chaperones walked in talking. They had no knowledge that I was also in the room. One said to another that she could not believe that 10-year-olds could understand and properly use the term inertia. The other continued by saying that her group had not only mastered identifying and correctly using all of Newton's Laws, but were even using potential and kinetic energy correctly. They were astounded that what they first thought was just a fun trip was one of the best learning experiences that they have seen in years. I did not emerge until they had left. But conversations like that reinforce to me that bringing pop culture into my curriculum has more pros than cons.

Did you know?

Pop culture themes are worldwide. Because of the Internet and travel, movies, music, literature, and more cross borders and oceans to be shared all over the world. http://www.learner.org/courses/worldhistory/support/activities_25.pdf

Ideas to Try

- **Create a safe and engaging learning environment**: This means do your research about pop culture before bringing it into your classroom. Don't let students use or view content that is inappropriate for them or for school. Keep their safety in mind. For example, when using social media remember these are still children and there are regulations that need to be followed. Don't post their names or give away any identity that could negatively impact the students.

- **Be an edutainer**: You are vying for the attention of the students and trying to find a way to share information in a meaningful way. You are the host, so-to-speak, of your classroom. While it would seem the teacher is less needed in the technological age, the truth is they are more important than ever to help students reach their full potential. Who else will be able to help students maximize their strengths, improve their social skills, and make the connection with the real world? I often say effective teachers understand the art of teaching as much as the science of teaching. Utilize your skills beyond the content knowledge of your subject. For example, one thing I enjoy is story telling. So whether I am teaching, public speaking, or simply conversing, I often share stories to make a point or connect to an important topic.

- **Create real-life, meaningful lessons** that help the students connect school to the real world. Create a product, including design, marketing, and commercials. Analyze and forecast profit of a business. Design a comic strip or children's book based upon the class or content area. Budget for a trip: gas prices vs. mileage, hotel costs vs. number of nights, etc. Build a blog where students can post poems or creative writings. Create a music video based upon a lesson. Create a video or video game to share content.

- **Give students a choice of assignments on a particular topic**, or ask them to design one of their own. When students are involved in designing the lesson, they better understand the goal of the lesson and become more emotionally invested in and attached to the learning outcomes. Be open to the use of pop culture within these projects. Songs, movies, literature, cartoons, or anything that is currently trending should be considered as a way to enhance the activity.

- **Start each day with movement**: One of the best ways to start each day, especially in elementary school is to have students stand up and move/ dance around to a song. This is a great way to get the heart pumping and help the students get the "wiggles" out of their systems. I (Brad) spent a month in Malaysia helping their Ministry of Education develop a fitness certification for their teachers. I actually got to spend a few weeks traveling throughout Malaysia speaking at various teaching centers. One of the activities their teachers shared with me was a warm up activity that they do every morning in their elementary schools with all of their students. On the televisions they would play videos such as Dora the

Explorer dancing to the song, "The Lion Sleeps Tonight." All of the students would stand up and move along with the dance steps as Dora the Explorer and her friends danced to the music too. The students loved it and looked forward to it every morning. Bringing music in that they enjoy as well as using the physical activity stimulates their brains and helps the students be ready to learn.

- **Incorporate technology** whenever possible. Allow students to create videos, songs, advertisements, and even products. Think of Khan Academy for example, which uses a variety of video lessons for their students. There is a plethora of online streaming companies that offer great video libraries at a fraction of the cost of purchasing videos. We use discovery education and love it! Based upon the age of the students and district policies, even social media, blogs, and other Internet services can be used to enhance the learning experience. These are tools that are used in the business world, so students need to develop their skills in using them as well.

- **Incorporate video games** into the learning. I'm not talking about games that focus only on the same "kill and drill" concepts that are used in the classroom, but games that allow students to think critically, strategize, explore, and create. In fact, the military, pilots, some businesses, and medical practices are incorporating video games into their professional learning and development. By the way, video gaming in 2012 earned $67 billion dollars worldwide and is expected to earn around $82 billion dollars annually by 2017. So, regardless of your personal view of video games, they are a major part of our culture and are being integrated into the business sector more each year.

- **Guest speakers** are another way to connect learning with the real world. While it would be great to have a CEO of a major corporation, a well-known professional athlete or famous celebrity to speak at your school, there are many people who would be great choices within any community. When I taught in the K–12 setting, I tried to get people from all different sectors to come speak to students at assemblies or even in individual classes. I was able to get people like eight-times Mr. Olympia Lee Haney, baseball CY Young Award Winner John Smoltz, and other such celebrities. But I also brought in the director of the local food bank, the mayor of our city, and other local business people who could share their knowledge and experiences with the student.

Key Points to Remember

- Edutaining is connecting the learning in the classroom to the real world in a fun and meaningful way.

- Edutainment (pop-culture) should enhance education, not be the primary aspect of education. Begin a new concept with a video clip or some other unique approach.

- When using pop-culture be sure it is age-appropriate and fits within any regulations the school has developed.

- Connect the lesson to real-world events (news, media, literature, songs, etc.). Examine why a sit-com or reality show is so successful. Make sure it is age and content appropriate.

- Bring in guest speakers (CEOs, athletes, celebrities, public figures).

Motivate Towards Excellence

"If you can imagine it, you can achieve it; if you can dream it, you can become it."

William Arthur Ward

Our Thoughts and Some Research Too

Motivation and achievement have long been recognized to have a close cause–effect relationship. Never has this relationship been more important than in today's culture. Educating students today is not about the lack of information but rather a lack of motivation. Through the Internet, iPods, cell phones, and other technology, students have continual access to information. Because of this access, many students aren't motivated much beyond simply finding information. This is true even at the collegiate level. As one college professor explained, "I have seen a dramatic increase in the number of students who will Google information to add to a research paper, but they don't bother to verify that it is a credible source or even the accuracy of the information." Regardless of age level, many students simply aren't motivated beyond doing the bare minimum of work. I have even had a student ask Siri for an answer. This work is then turned in with an expectation that it is acceptable because they did after all turn in something.

Students live, learn, and play in a media-saturated society, in a world of "edutainment" and spectacle. For many students formal curriculum seems irrelevant and they become disengaged from learning. So, how do you motivate students who seem more interested in whether or not someone is voted off a dance show or eaten by a zombie than if they learn math? How do you help them experience excellence in education and life?

First, give students an opportunity to use their talents to achieve success by developing their strengths. This may mean giving them an interest inventory or just by making observations throughout the year. When you see a student excel in an area then give them the opportunity to continue the growth. I always have students who excel in drawing and the Arts, but don't always have ways to use them within the assignments. I try to incorporate ways and let them use and develop their talents. It may be as simple as drawing the vocabulary term in action instead of writing the definition. To that student, the drawing makes just as much sense and helps them excel even more in an area in which they can become truly excellent.

This is why it is important to relate lessons to their lives. Find areas of strength and incorporate them into the lessons when possible. While they are engaged in these successful tasks, we can help them to learn how to improve other skills in an environment where the child cares about doing a good job. This doesn't mean that a child should never fail, because children can develop an improved self-concept through struggle. However, if failure is all that a student continually experiences then self-esteem and motivation both decrease significantly, never allowing the students to experience excellence.

Offering choices is also a great motivational method. This helps develop ownership in the learning process. Often in groups for science we have numerous jobs. There are times when I will let the students choose their jobs. This simple choice gives them the buy-in to perform well in that specific area. When the child makes decisions he is more likely to accept ownership and control of the results. This sense of control fosters responsibility. However, always offer choices that are equally acceptable to you. By providing choices, they learn to value themselves and their own decision-making ability.

Like it or not, reward systems do have their place in every aspect of life. Parents often reward children with gifts or money for good grades. Even as adults we like to be recognized or rewarded. These rewards could be everything from a verbal "attaboy" or a certificate of recognition to winning the Oscar in the category "Teacher of the Year." We all like the "extra" motivations we can sometimes earn. Giving the student a simple comment to recognize positive behavior or having the work published on a bulletin board are realistic and meaningful rewards. This doesn't mean students should be rewarded for everything. Rewards when used out of context—for example, as a way to get the class to be quiet—actually show a lack of management. Rewards are most effective when used with lower ability or unmotivated students when the reward is used for a short time only. In a classroom, where the teacher can motivate and connect with the students, the real reward for good work will eventually become the satisfaction derived from hard work.

Finally, create a nurturing environment that will permit children to fail without penalty. Isn't this what video games are? The people who play can lose a life or not reach the next level with the knowledge that they just get to try again without a real penalty. My (Julie) son will play the same level for what seems like hours and still want to play the next day. What if we let students retake tests until they have mastered the content? Instead of focusing on the failure, won't the students possibly want to try again knowing they can reach the next level? Learning how to deal with failure is critical for developing motivation and successful learning. Students should learn that they can and must learn from their mistakes. Failure is actually a learning tool. This is an important concept that parents can reinforce with the students at home as well. Learning from failure is an important part of future success.

Great coaches continually challenge their athletes to do better and to push their limits towards excellence, not accepting mediocrity. One way that great coaches inspire their athletes to believe in themselves is by continually putting them in situations that challenge them. That is, they are pushing their athletes outside of their comfort zone, physically, mentally, and emotionally. When athletes are successful when pushed to their limits, they then are willing to push even further. This builds confidence in their ability to handle tough situations. This is sometimes called the "Get Comfortable Being Uncomfortable principle." The only way to grow physically and emotionally is to constantly challenge yourself to do things that aren't easy. It is the same concept as a muscle growing when it is pushed to the limit and challenged.

Dr. Alan Goldberg, noted psychologist, believes that the best coaches do not allow their players to just get by with the status quo. They refuse to tolerate mediocrity in effort, attitude, technique, training or performance. Because they continually challenge their athletes, they are able to keep them highly motivated. There is nothing more motivating to an athlete than being challenged, experiencing themselves successfully rising to meet that test and as a result, improving. When coaches fail to adequately challenge their athletes, when they instead allow them to remain stagnating within their comfort zone, they will ultimately end up losing those athletes to boredom and apathy.

Now take the word "coach" out of every statement from above and replace it with teacher. Then change "sport" to classroom. Re-read the section and try it! Doesn't it still make sense? A teacher is a coach within the classroom. The sport is our subject area and the students are our athletes. Here is how the first section will read:

Great **teachers** continually challenge their **students** to do better and push their limits towards excellence not accepting mediocrity. One way that great **teachers** inspire their **students** to believe in themselves is by continually putting them in situations that challenge their limiting beliefs. That is, these **teachers** are always pushing their **students** outside of their comfort zone, physically, mentally and emotionally, and then helping them discover that, in fact, they can do better than they first believed they could. These **teachers** teach the "Get Comfortable Being Uncomfortable principle." To them, the only way to grow physically and emotionally is to constantly challenge yourself to do things that aren't easy, to attempt things that truly stretch you.

The best **teachers** do not allow their **students** to just get by with the status quo. They refuse to tolerate mediocrity in effort, attitude, technique, training or performance. Because they continually challenge their **students**, they are able to keep them highly motivated. There is nothing more motivating to a **student** than being challenged, experiencing themselves successfully rising to meet that test and as a result, improving. When **teachers** fail to adequately challenge their **students**, when they instead allow them to remain stagnating within their comfort zone, they will ultimately end up losing those **students** to boredom and apathy.

Do you see the connection? Is thinking our classroom is like an athletic field beneficial to our students? Those who have experience being a coach or an athlete can make this connection and motivate to bring excellence into the classroom just as a coach would to the athletic field.

However, regardless of the failed initiatives, misguided politicians, and relentless testing, which have all hindered education, there are still classrooms full of effective teachers who instill excellence in their students. As a former state superintendent, Kathy Cox, explains, "Nothing is more important to the student's success than a positive relationship with the teacher regardless of interferences to their education such as a tough home life, limited parental support or socioeconomic level." This means developing positive relationships with students and creating an engaging learning environment. An engaging learning environment creates an environment where students can excel, not just meet minimum standards. Don't all of our children deserve the chance to be excellent?

Engaging in excellence means more than test preparation, delivering random facts, and giving fragmented information. Remember students are inundated with information from a multitude of sources. Excellence in education requires distinguishing what information is important, and how to apply the information to the lives of the students and future learning. You are the leader in your classroom, whether it be as a coach or whatever means works for you. Striving for excellence is the key! Help your students reach levels they never thought were possible!

Did you know?

Students resent the idea of being influenced and told what to do. By making the learning meaningful they will become more motivated. https://college.cengage.com/education/pbl/tc/motivate.html

Personal Experiences and Stories

One reason I (Julie) am a teacher now is because of teachers I have had growing up. I have had awe-inspiring teachers who have motivated me to work hard and experience success. I can tell you about teachers who introduced music into literature lessons, who motivated me to dissect frogs, and who even encouraged me to pursue my passion to be a teacher. But it is the one who didn't that I remember just as clearly.

While I was in high school I took an AP chemistry and physics course. I was one of only a few girls in the male-dominated course and interested in a field of study that not many other girls were. Needless to say, I never ended up pursuing that field of study. Today I happen to be thankful for that because I love being a teacher, but at the time it was hard for me to understand.

It is over 25 years later and I still can picture the teacher and see the event happening again. I can picture the science classroom, the lab table, and see the ball rolling off the table. I can still see the tall, male figure in a sweater and tie standing over me. One day in AP Chemistry/Physics class we were conducting a lab where we rolled a ball across the table that made dots on a large piece of paper. We were calculating speed and velocity. I apparently rolled my ball a little too hard and it flew off the lab table. The teacher promptly came over and reprimanded me for my carelessness. He told me he didn't appreciate my free spirit and that I had too much energy to take anything seriously in the course. He proceeded to tell me that women didn't belong in the science field and that I should just plan on being barefoot and pregnant in a kitchen instead of being in a lab. I responded that it took a real man to be a teacher and that he needed to learn better teaching skills. I was kicked out of that class and sent to the Dean.

As I sat in the Dean's office I realized that how I responded was very disrespectful, but what I realized even more than that was the fact that I was being told I could not do something. That infuriated me. He had no intention in helping me succeed nor did the teacher want me to experience success. He had no intention of motivating me or encouraging me. He wanted to prove that boys were superior to girls in the field of science. I remember the Dean trying to explain that not many girls qualify for the class and that the teacher was going to have to get used to more and more girls being involved in science. I was stunned about the whole situation. I had always had caring, nurturing teachers until then. I remained in his class out of spite, and eventually lost the passion for that field of science. The lack of motivation and encouragement for excellence impacted me in ways that would stay with me forever.

When students realize they have certain strengths and a desire to develop them, then excellence is something they are dedicated to work toward. I (Brad) have trained many athletes who had the talent and desire to compete in collegiate sports. While I have coached most sports at some point during my teaching career, I have mainly worked with athletes on strength and conditioning and of course developing their leadership skills. Excellence is really nothing more than someone investing the time to develop their strengths to their maximum potential. To paraphrase Aristotle, excellence is not an act, but rather it is a habit. I was able to help these student athletes with their work habits, goal setting, and leadership skills. With hard work and dedication, most of these athletes attained their goal of playing athletics at the collegiate level.

What has impressed me the most about these student athletes is not their athletic ability, but their desire for excellence and their commitment to achieving it. These athletes have performed well on the field, in the classroom, and been leaders on their teams as well. Now imagine if we put that effort into helping every child maximize their talents and provide opportunities for them to reach their goals. School would no longer be seen as boring or a waste of time, but it would be a place students would want to come and grow.

Did you know?

Students want to do activities "out of the box" and that go beyond the norm. http://www.educationworld.com/a_curr/columnists/mcdonald/mcdonald007.shtml

Ideas to Try

Consider these strategies for motivating the students throughout the school year:

- Praise students on specific behavior. Be sure to tell them exactly what is being praised and that will motivate the students to continue that behavior.
- Use tools in technology that the students know how to use. It will build self-esteem and motivate them as well since it is a familiar format of information. If teachers don't use technology because they are not proficient in it, allow the students to be the experts.
- Reinforce hard work with public praise and occasionally a reward or privilege.
- Provide opportunities for a variety of experiences, like field trips.
- Make lessons as applicable to the real world as possible, such as using grocery shopping for math content.
- Make students active participants in learning, such as making videos or teaching class.
- Treat students with respect.
- Inspire students to do their best. Students really do want to succeed.

Here are a few strategies for bringing excellence back to education:

- Have high expectations of all students. Students typically want to please their teacher if they feel a connection with her.
- Help students find their passions and make your passion for learning contagious to them.

- Create an environment of risk taking. Failure is actually a learning tool.
- Instill a strong work ethic in students. Motto "Work Hard, Play Hard."
- Help students set short-term and long-term goals (academic, social, etc.).
- Focus on characteristics that will make them successful in life (leadership, creativity, perseverance, respect, responsibility, etc.).
- Move beyond information. Information is everywhere, but students need to learn what is quality information and they need to learn how to use the information. This involves application of knowledge, but it also requires critical thinking skills to analyze information.
- Challenge yourself to be a better teacher by going to training and learning the advancements within your field of education.
- Hang inspirational sayings in the classroom.

Key Points to Remember

- Every student has the potential to experience success.
- Motivating students can come in many forms and is essential for student success.
- Failing is OK. Teach students how to learn from failing. Create a safe environment where students feel like they can take certain risks.
- Use appropriate praise to encourage students.
- Students are motivated by their interests. Help them build on their interests and passions and they will strive for excellence.
- Expose students to more than subject content, such as art, music, and even physical fitness activities. This can be a powerful motivator to some students.
- Challenge your students so they feel a sense of accomplishment. Remember a muscle only grows when it works against resistance.
- Excellence is created through good habits. Reinforce this concept often.

Hold Students Accountable and Responsible

"It is wrong and immoral to seek to escape the consequences of one's acts."

Mahatma Gandhi

Our Thoughts and Some Research Too

Who's Doing the Work Anyway?

Have you ever received a project from a student that looked like an engineer from MIT built it? What about an essay that is so perfectly written that it could be published? Do you question who has completed a student's homework? If you have taught long enough then you can probably relate to the scenario of questioning who actually completed the work that was assigned to the student. The first thought you may have is: did the student really do this work? While you know the answer, and you know that parents know you know the answer, you are amazed the student would turn it in and take the credit for the work. Worse than that, you are amazed that the parents would encourage it. At the end you are torn with how to grade the work that was clearly done by, or with a great amount of help from, the parents.

How can we hold students accountable and accurately assess the work if the parents are doing the work? How do we help the students own their learning process and understand accountability? Do parents realize that when they do the work for their child they are overstepping their boundaries and not allowing for a proper assessment, which means they are actually doing their child a disservice? How do we as educators instill responsibility in both the parents and the students? How do we educate them on their roles in the learning process?

What is Your Role in the Educational Process?

Educating a child takes a team. Teachers, students, and parents must all work together in order to create the best learning environment. This takes communication, trust, and knowing each other's roles. The teachers are the primary facilitator with their main role as providing the opportunity to learn. The parents are the main supporters within the team. The students are the team players and have to be willing to put forth effort, work hard, and take responsibility. While these roles may appear simple and seem to make sense, they are not the current roles played in many classrooms today. Teachers often stand in front of the class and give knowledge, hence being given the power and the responsibility to transfer their knowledge to the students. The students are expected to sit quietly and receive the information with the expectation to take it all in. The parents take over at home and often give instructions different from the teacher.

When this occurs the students are stuck in the middle and are often made to choose which side to take. The students become spectators in their own learning process. The concept of teachers being the givers of the knowledge and the students being the receivers takes away all notions of responsibility for the students and puts the responsibility solely on the teachers. It leaves the parents out all together. While the team concept may seem like a paradigm shift to some, it is essential to recognize that the learning process is about the students experiencing success and the educational journey that they will take.

Understanding the roles of all team members is crucial to the success of the team. In this team setting, the teacher is the facilitator within a team environment, not the dictator or lone giver of knowledge. The parents and the students are part of this team and both have important roles, too. The primary role of the parents is to support the teachers and the students. The parents become a partner within the learning process and are there as a support to teachers in ways that provide the opportunity for the student to learn. They also support the student and help in any way they need it, but respect that this is the student's journey and not their own. These boundaries need to be clearly communicated within the team. If an assignment is to be done by the student, then that should be communicated with the parent and the student. The parent then should respect the teacher's request and give the student the opportunity to work on his or her own.

Homework is a perfect example of this. Homework gives the teacher immediate feedback on how well the student understands a concept. If the teacher gets inaccurate feedback because the parent has done the work, then the learning process has been compromised and the student cannot flourish as needed. While meaning well, that is when the parent helping is actually a disservice. It is when the parents step into the role of the student and take over a project that it is really harming the educational progress of the student. Often parents want their child to receive a good grade, but receiving is very different than earning. When parents do the work then the students don't learn. They don't learn the material, but they also don't experience the process that one goes through when completing a project. The struggle, sense of accomplishment and finally the feeling of success are also part of the learning experience. Parents usually have the student's best interest in mind and don't realize that they are actually harming the learning process by doing the work for their child.

Interestingly, research suggests that US parents are more involved with their children's homework than in any other country. The data revealed that 79 percent of fourth grader parents in the US set aside time for homework on a daily basis as compared to 70 percent of students worldwide. However, only 25 percent of Japanese students and 22 percent of South Korean students reported that their parents made them set aside daily homework time. Whether or not it is cultural norms, an emphasis on grades or some other reason, it is clear that parents take on more responsibility than parents in other countries for their students' learning. However, considering US tests scores in comparison to these other countries, are they really helping their children?

Teaching responsibility for the role of parent and especially the students is essential to the teamwork aspect. Each team member has his or her own responsibilities to adhere to within their roles. It is the teacher's responsibility to facilitate the learning environment in the best way possible for all students to learn. This goes beyond being academically qualified to teach the content area. That is the basis, but there is so much more. The teacher is responsible for getting to know each student, developing a personal relationship with each student, creating a safe and caring learning environment, developing a relationship with parents, communicating regularly and effectively with students and parents, and presenting the content in a meaningful way to accommodate all learning styles and differences.

The student has the responsibility to take ownership in his or her own learning process. While that does mean behaving appropriately and showing up to class, it also means being an active and productive member of the classroom. Students should participate, ask questions when they have them, and also put forth effort to complete any and all work. They should communicate with teachers and parents if they are in need of help or are struggling. They need to know their voice is respected and that they are the most important aspect in the learning team. Parents have the role of being supporters to both the students and the teachers. They should have an open line of communication with their child and the teacher and know the boundaries that should be set in regards to doing work with or for their child. When all team members clearly understand their roles and responsibilities then the team has the potential to experience success and have an exceptional learning journey.

Communication between teachers, parents, and students is a vital aspect in this teamwork concept. When teachers communicate their expectations and goals with the students and parents then they all can understand their roles and be effective team members. Children are more likely to be motivated to achieve if they get the same clear and positive message about school effort and expectations from both parents and teachers. Communication between teacher and parents in front of a child dramatically affects children's behaviors and self-perceptions. When we conference in our lower school, grades 1–5, we invite the students to be a part of the conference. There are times when adult talk is necessary, but there are times when the students should be a part of the conference. We sit as a team and talk about progress and goals. Teachers and parents don't talk *about* a student instead they all talk together. Starting in middle school, grade 6, the students actually run the conference and they assume the facilitator role. They are responsible for knowing their grades and communicating goals that have been set. This continues all the way through grade 12 with the students also having a say in their course selection. It is amazing how the students take pride and own their goals as well as their academic achievement.

This past year my own child, who was in tenth grade, came home with his class choices for eleventh grade. I (Julie) was in shock and voiced my concern, but he stated his reasons and I trusted that he was making the right choices. I was not a fan of three advanced placements classes and two honors classes with an overload and no study hall. But he had been responsible for his class schedule so far and he knew what he wanted to accomplish. That was when I, as a parent, had to let my child take the lead. I will be there to support my child, but ultimately his work is his responsibility. I have to remember that I am part of a team and that it is my child's educational journey, not mine.

How Do We Teach Accountability?

Being held accountable means taking responsibility and owning your actions. Responsibility and accountability go hand-in-hand and without one you cannot experience the other. When there is a lack of responsibility then blame occurs. Have you ever wrongly blamed someone for something or has there been a time when you should have taken the blame, but did not? It all centers on responsibility. If someone had owned the behavior then blame would never have occurred. Blame often equates with hurt feelings and can promote a negative learning environment.

To avoid playing the blame game, we need to promote a culture where team members are held accountable and are responsible. For this to occur there must be clear roles established along with expectations and consequences. Each team member must be held accountable for performing their established role to the best of their ability. This can be done with self-evaluations and open communication. The expectations and consequences must be agreed upon by all of the team members. This will insure buy-in by all team members and help promote a unified learning environment. I often have learning contracts where all of the team members meet to discuss the roles and responsibilities. We all sign it and enter into an agreement. This helps us with the accountability aspect.

Accountability is often a challenging concept when dealing with different ages and genders. Students who are younger have to be given different roles and responsibilities than students who are older. Parents experience a generational difference and have a hard time understanding their role because it is very different from when they were in school. Boys tend to have a different role within certain cultures and communities than the girls have. Being aware of all of these differences is crucial to the understanding and establishing of the accountability roles within the learning teams.

Should students age 6 be held accountable in the same way as 16 year olds? Absolutely not! We as teachers need to keep in mind developmentally appropriate lessons and opportunities to teach responsibility and accountability. This often equates with the consequences that go along with being held accountable. There are times when the lesson should be learning from the act and then there are times when the consequences should be more severe. If a 6-year-old forgets a book then she can call home or bring it the next day. While if a 16-year-old forgets a book then she may receive a late fee or a deduction of points. The 16-year-old has already been given the chances to learn the lesson and experience consequences that go along with accountability while the 6-year-old has not yet been given those chances. I often do something I call "rewind" with my students, who average around 10 years old. If they do something they should not then I say, "rewind." This is a cue for them to go back and do the correct thing. This not only shows them they have done something wrong, but it also allows them to model the correct behavior and learn from the situation.

The classroom that you step foot in is very different from the classroom in which you walked in when you were a student. The classroom you walked into when you were a student is very different from which your parents stepped into. You need to keep that generational aspect in the back of your mind as you focus on responsibility and accountability. My parents were totally hands-off with my education and expected the teacher to be the giver of the knowledge. There were only parent conferences if we got in trouble. There were no learning communities or team concepts. When they were in school it was even more hands-off than that. There has been a paradigm shift in regards to the learning environment. My parents never were accountable for any aspect of my education when I was a child. Therefore they did not model the role that I, as a parent, am being asked to play. The roles and responsibilities are very different within the educational setting than they were even a generation ago. Recognizing these differences between the generations is essential to the success of the team structure.

Teaching accountability with the male gender is very different from teaching the female students. Boys today often don't understand accountability because they tend to equate it with success and status within the community instead of being personally responsible for actions. It is like they are held to higher standards and are not being given the opportunity to learn how to be held accountable. It is almost like it is just expected of them. Boys are competitive by nature and most grow up within societies where they are expected to be the breadwinners and provide for their families. Parents know that their children will be competing for jobs on a global scale and they almost expect them to have a drive and desire that they are too young to even understand. There is an enormous amount of pressure put on boys to succeed and to become responsible men.

While girls also have to learn about responsibility and accountability there is still a traditional mindset that boys should be the head of the family and take care of the home financially. This, to me, is archaic, but it is a mindset that we as teachers cannot ignore. This can make it even harder for females and for parents of females. They want their daughters to have the same opportunities as males. In this day and age there are still cultures where girls do not have the same rites and opportunities. This was the basis for Title IX legislation in universities years ago. Thousands of studies have been conducted about gender equality. But girls still need to prove themselves and unfortunately this can also mean that the parents become too involved in the education process and don't allow opportunities for their daughters to experience failure and learn responsibility. If females are going to have an equal part in society, then they need to learn responsibility and accountability just as males students do.

Did you know?

Teachers are the most influential aspect of the classroom. Students will perform better if they feel a connection with the teacher. https://www.apa.org/education/k12/relationships.aspx

Personal Experiences and Stories

Just One Example of Many Where Parents Do Work for Their Children

One year I (Julie) actually had a parent build a trebuchet for a science project for his child. While I understand that it requires adult supervision with the tools, this parent took it too far. When the child was presenting his report the parent also stood up to talk. When it came time to launch, the parent wouldn't even let the child launch it or touch it. It was clear who did the work and it was even more obvious who was harmed in the process. I proceeded to give the parent a grade along with his son. The really sad part was that he appreciated me noticing his effort to help his son. He loved that he got a grade, too. After the entire situation occurred we all sat down and discussed the project. While it was a hard conversation to have, it was necessary. We discussed all of our roles and responsibilities. We also discussed accountability. The parent admitted he had his son's best interest in mind and he really wanted him to get a good grade. We all agreed at the end that the student have another opportunity to do his own project. His dad was more than welcome to help with tools, if needed, but the student needed to do the work. By the end of this situation everyone learned something about responsibility and accountability.

A Glimpse into a Learning Community that Promotes Responsibility and Accountability

Imagine walking into a classroom where the first words, after greeting the students, which the teacher says are, "OK, get to work" and you observe students all engaged working at lab tables on a scientific experiment. You quickly learn that the students are in the middle of a lab experiment that is being continued from the day before. The students clearly understand the procedures and what is expected of them. They are responsible for their lab materials and are being held accountable with respect to being able to continue the lab from one day to the next. You continue to observe the teacher walking around and interacting with the individual groups. You hear the students ask questions freely and then you witness conversations that challenge a student's thinking and have them wanting to find out answers on their own. He does not do the work for the students; he is teaching them that they are responsible for their own learning. The teacher undoubtedly respects each and every student within the classroom. This is a typical day within my son's science class.

My (Julie) son is currently 14 years old and he recognizes his teacher, Jason Fricker, as a partner in his learning process. He goes on to share that "Mr. Fricker doesn't lecture to the class like he knows it all and that we have to learn it and that Mr. Fricker will even tell the class to let him know if he is starting to talk too long." How amazing is that? The main focus in that classroom is the students and their learning, not how much the teacher knows or how he can cram information into the heads of the students. My son describes him as almost being one of the students. He said that Mr. Fricker clearly is the teacher of the class, but that he gives credit to the students' ideas. He actually gives the students a voice, listens, and respects what they have to say. This makes the students feel valued and creates an environment where they are vested in their own learning and want to do well. I have had the opportunity to observe Mr. Fricker's science class on different occasions and Mr. Fricker is continually challenging and engaging the students in the science content. He helps the students to be responsible and accountable for their own learning by creating meaningful activities for the students to complete.

My son is hoping to make it to the advanced science class for the next school year. When I talked with Mr. Fricker about this he shared that if my son was truly accountable for his own work and that his work was 100 percent his own that he would support him in the decision. I was talking to him as a parent first, but I also tend to revert my thinking back to being a teacher. As a teacher I respected and understood this statement. I recognize that parents often help students a little too much which doesn't give a true sense of the student's potential or ability. As a parent I appreciated this statement even more. I knew that Mr. Fricker had my child's best interest in mind. He wanted to make sure my son was responsible and could be held accountable for the level of work an advanced class would entail. I could easily say that, without a doubt, my son's work was his own and that he was learning to be accountable for his own education. With Mr. Fricker I feel like part of a team. Together we all want what is best for my son and will support him and help him reach his goals along the way.

Did you know?

Students respond to accountability when there is a cause and effect relationship. They need to see why being accountable is important in order to put forth the effort. http://www.studygs.net/attmot2.htm

Ideas to Try

- **Establish a team**: This takes planning time and often time within the schedules to make the team concept work. Once this is established then you can hold a meeting at the beginning of the school year with the parents and students and set the groundwork for a team model to be used within the classroom. Share expectations and goals for the school year that are associated with being a team. Also share roles and responsibilities of each team member. Some teachers even have a contract to be signed to seal the deal. Once the initial buy-in occurs set up individual conferences throughout the year to reinforce and enhance the team that you have established.

- **Use teachable moments to learn responsibility**: There are moments at any age level where students do not model appropriate responsibility. Use this as a teachable moment and share it with the class. You can use made-up scenarios or actual scenarios that happen within your class. If using a specific student, be sure to have the student's approval and make the outcome positive. If students can have the opportunity to experience and learn from real life situations then they are more than likely going to make a personal connection with learning responsibility and accountability.

- **Give opportunities for responsibility**: Students should be responsible for their own materials and area. This includes desks at which they sit and lockers where they keep their materials. In my homeroom we have a locker fairy that secretly visits and leaves little treats for those who are organized and show responsibility for having a clean area. This may also be creating a simple job like passing out papers, taking attendance, feeding the animals, or anything that can give the students a little extra opportunity to learn about responsibility. It is a great idea to have class discussions about what happens if that job is not done and how to hold the students accountable for their actions.

- **Set goals**: By having short and long-term goals the students can experience how hard work pays off. This will help instill responsibility and also hold the students accountable for reaching a certain objective of their own personal interest.

- **Provide clear instructions to who should be doing the work**: Be sure to communicate with parents and students when and how much a parent should be helping. Remember parents often have their child's best interest in mind and may not realize they are doing them a disservice by helping or doing their work.

- **Create a culture where the student role mimics a job in the real world**: My husband has told both of our boys that their only job right now is to be a student. Sports, games, and all other interests are secondary. He equates being a student to real life and having a job. If the boys perform well, then just like in the work place, they are rewarded. For them this means that they can participate in extra-curricular activities. If they do not perform as expected, then there are consequences. He is teaching our boys to be accountable for their own education. He is also teaching them real-life skills. He wants them to be able to take care of a family and be a productive member of society. Using this mindset with students in the classroom will help them to understand the importance of learning responsibility and accountability.

- **Let students play an active role in their learning**: This means let the students choose topics, groups, or find a way for them to have a say in their own learning process. This way you are guaranteed buy-in from the student, which means they are more likely to be responsible for their work.

- **Praise and recognize responsible acts**: While this may almost seem too simple, it is important. Both students and parents need positive, meaningful feedback on their roles and responsibilities. Praise specific actions and recognize the positive behaviors that will promote responsibility and accountability.

- **Have clear consequences for when students do not model accountability**: Be sure to create age-appropriate consequences for the students. It is a good idea to have the students be a part of the establishment of the consequences. They are more likely to understand and recognize them if they are part of the design process. Then communicate these consequences with parents and students. Also, be sure to follow through with the consequences. If students see that there are no consequences then they will never have the need to be accountable.

- **Example of a study tool to teach responsibility**: Before each major test we, as a class, set up a review plan. I call this activity Teaching Parents. It is stemmed from the idea that if a child can teach a concept then he/she has mastered the concept. This usually includes a weeklong study chart with the student having homework each night. Each topic is broken up to where the students should study 10–15 minutes on each concept. Note that the students help with the design of the study chart, so they are vested in what is being studied. They also create a list of the materials they will need. This is written after the chart. After the studying for the night, they need to teach their parents the concept. This shows responsibility that the students have learned/studied the content prior to the teaching. The students come up with their own creative ways to teach their parents. I have heard stories of quizzes being given and conversations at dinner tables. It is whatever works best for the students and their families. Numerous people have commented on how this activity has helped students learn responsibility. Our learning service specialist has asked that other teachers also use this format. Parents have shared that students have used this model for classes taken years after they have left mine. Students have shared feedback that they like that they are the ones in charge!

Key Points to Remember

- Establish a team with clear and meaningful roles and guidelines.

- Communicate with all team members as often as needed.

- Give students the opportunity to learn responsibility.

- Create lessons and activities where the students can be vested in their work.

- Use goal setting to help the students experience responsibility and accountability.

- Give feedback and praise as well as have meaningful consequences.

- Beyond rules, have high expectations for your students. I believe that students will always rise to your lowest expectations, so make them high.

- Establish a sense of purpose. Help students understand how working hard and doing well in school will help them improve their lives and maximize their future options.

- Emphasize that great leaders take responsibility for their actions, they don't make excuses.

10 | Foster Perseverance and the Ability to Learn from Failure

"Life's greatest lessons are learned in the midst of life's greatest struggles."

Dr. James Merritt

Our Thoughts and Some Research Too

Have you ever started a diet only to give up on it within a few weeks or even a few days? You started out with the best of intentions but within a short period of time, you fell off the wagon and you ate that chocolate cake that had been calling your name! However, rather than focus on the hard work you had done for three or four weeks, you focused on the empty plate where only the crumbs of the chocolate cake remained and ultimately felt like a failure. How did you handle the situation? Did you let the negative feelings win, declare yourself a failure, and immediately pull out the ice cream? Or did you realize it was nothing but a tasty treat that wouldn't keep you from your goals and refocus your efforts to do even better?

To be successful on a diet or any other endeavor, it takes not only perseverance, but implementing strategies that will help the perseverance pay off. Perseverance is, after all, the foundation of excellence. That's right; if students want to achieve excellence then they have to learn to persevere. An important aspect of perseverance is using strategies to help cope with failure and become resilient in tough times.

If you have ever failed at something, well then you are in good company. Walt Disney was fired from a newspaper job because the editor told him that he lacked imagination and had no good ideas. Winston Churchill struggled in school and failed the sixth grade. After school Churchill faced many years of political failures, as he was defeated in every election for public office until he finally became the Prime Minister at the young age of 62. Henry Ford's early businesses failed and left him broke five times before he founded the successful Ford Motor Company. Even the classic book *Lord of the Flies* was rejected by two dozen publishers with one publisher responding to Mr. Golding by calling the book rubbish and absurd. But did these people give up? No, and countless others have their own stories of triumph after many failures. What did they all have in common? They failed, time and time again! But they never gave up; they persevered!

What helped them overcome their failures and to be resilient during tough times? Was it their superior intellect? Was it their ability to take a standardized test? Probably not. More than likely they were able to reflect on things they did well versus things that didn't go well and make adjustments. There is a term we now know as emotional intelligence that some experts believe is just as important as IQ (intellectual quotient) in attaining success in life. Emotional intelligence is the ability to perceive, control, and evaluate emotions. Emotional intelligence can be learned and strengthened just like any other skill set. As you may have recognized, the theme throughout the book is to develop skills that will help students excel in the real world. Learning to evaluate and control our emotions can be critical to success in life, but it may also be just as important for students in academia as well. What if students learned to control and manage their emotions when enduring difficulties or even failures? Could this be one of the keys to them excelling in the classroom and beyond?

Unfortunately many students may never accomplish great things because they won't endure difficulties long enough to experience them. Think of the quote above, "Life's greatest lessons are learned in the midst of life's greatest struggles." What a profound way to look at perseverance. This means some of life's greatest lessons and some of life's greatest accomplishments can only be experienced through tough times and hard work. Unfortunately, we live in a culture where students seem to have a sense of entitlement with the expectation of instant gratification. If something seems hard then they either avoid it, or assume that any work they provide should be adequate. After all, they did try, so that should be good enough. Plain and simple, the students don't have the tools they need to persevere because they have never been taught them.

Perseverance equates with having a good work ethic. Think back to that thing you started but did not finish. Should you have stuck with it? Maybe?

Maybe not. Now transfer that to the classroom. What are the times that students need to gut it out and finish? The first thing that comes to mind is standardized tests. Students need to stay focused long enough to complete the tests. This is often harder than it sounds. I have watched students put heads on desks, stare around the room, twirl pencils, draw in booklets, and ask to get water or use the bathroom. They come up with all kinds of excuses so they don't have to finish the test. As a teacher, I need to help them prepare for this type of situation and help them learn how to have a strong work ethic and persevere through the test.

Do students always need to finish everything they start? Do they need to persevere through everything? Not necessarily. That is also an important concept to teach students. The best example I can give is writing an essay. Students don't take every piece to the publication stage and that is all right. We use the writer's workshop model in our lower school, which teaches the students the writing process from brainstorming through publication. Teachers conference with students regularly and help the students figure out if they want to persevere through the entire process with the topic they are using. If so, then they continue with the writing. If not, then they find a new topic to begin. The teacher does require finished pieces (the number depends on the student), so every student must show a good work ethic and complete the writing process. But they are able to do this because of teacher encouragement and because they understand the purpose of having to persevere.

Another aspect of persevering is dealing with failure. Do students really know how to fail? Do they accept failure? Do they quit because they fail? Another disservice we have done to children is to try and keep them from ever experiencing failure. We have made the word "fail" so offensive that many see it as the F-word. But aren't we doing children a disservice by giving it such a negative connotation? In schools with so much focus put on standardized tests and grades, we have created a culture where failure is feared. In fact, we have created a culture where children worry more about not failing rather than being successful. Just as we focus on areas of weakness rather than strengths, we tend to focus more on failure or fear of failure rather than on being successful. We make things easier and we promote mediocrity as acceptable.

Even within schools, the focus is on students meeting a minimum level on tests, rather than seeking to excel. Rather than fearing failure, we actually need to help students become resilient in overcoming struggles and learning from failure. We need to provide them with the skills to focus on excelling rather than simply "not" failing. Part of changing their mind set deals with attitude.

Often this means students aren't willing to stick to it and continue putting forth effort when a challenge arises and they have difficulty performing a task. Failure then comes to be seen as negative rather than a learning opportunity. However, as we saw earlier, some of the most successful people only became successful after enduring many setbacks and failures. It is actually in the struggle that we learn valuable lessons that help us to be ultimately successful. That is what we need to be teaching our students. Think of the caterpillar in the cocoon. It is nice and comfortable in the cocoon. Yet, to become a butterfly it has to break out of the cocoon. Interestingly, it is the struggle to break out of the cocoon that strengthens the wings of the butterfly so it can fly. What if students could strengthen their coping skills, and see failure as a learning opportunity rather than as defeat?

Nationally recognized sports psychologist, Dr. Caroline Silby, says that one of the problems is that children lack an understanding of how to persevere. When speaking to students, she asks them what percentage of their outcome, such as in sports, is affected by their attitude. Usually students will say 50–100 percent. Next she will ask how much time they spend working on their attitude. The answer is usually never. So, if attitude is so important, why don't they spend time working on it? As Dr. Silby says, "They usually have no idea how to work on their attitude." Even many adults lack the skill set to work through tough times and to be resilient in failure.

While attitude may not seem like it is important, it really does make a difference when it comes to perseverance and failure versus success. In the Olympics for instance, research suggests there is only a 3 percent gap in performance/ability between medal winners and athletes who didn't even make the Olympic team. A 3 percent gap means that their physical abilities are very closely matched. This also means that the ability to handle stress, and utilize coping skills can be the difference between making the team and winning a medal. The difference between winning a medal and not even making the team has very little to do with their physical abilities, but has everything to do with their attitude and mental state of mind.

Now consider how students stress out about performing on standardized tests. What if the difference between high performing and low performing students isn't about mental ability, but the ability to handle stress and utilize coping skills to perform better? Think about how many students are diagnosed with test anxiety. Why is this? What can we do to help them overcome the stress? Do we ever focus on bringing these strategies into the classroom to help improve students' academic performances? Even athletes who learn how to cope and use strategies when they are competing may not recognize that these same skills can be transferred into the classroom for academic performance. While these strategies will be discussed more in-depth in the "ideas to share" section, some of the skills include anxiety reduction, positive self-talk, and goal setting. Once students understand that they can overcome failure and setbacks, they are more confident and willing to take on more risks to be successful. It is about students learning to take control of their situations/environment and creating a positive outcome.

Finally, an important skill related to perseverance and coping is the ability to make good decisions. Decision making is one area where students often have limited experience. Whether it is school, home, or extracurricular activities, students' days and activities are often set for them. There is not a lot of decision making they have to do. This means when they are presented with a problem, they may not be equipped to make good decisions and therefore have to deal with negative consequences. But imagine if students were better equipped with better decision-making skills.

Former NBA basketball star AC Green has often shared that when he was younger he would spend time in the gym practicing basketball rather than out partying with his friends on the weekends. He was once asked why he would spend time practicing when he could be out having fun. He told them that partying wasn't going to get him where he wanted to go, but that practicing would help him achieve his goal of playing college basketball. He not only played college basketball but he played in the NBA for 16 years. The decisions he made as a boy greatly influenced his success in school, college, basketball, and in life.

Perseverance, just like any other quality, has to be developed. People, especially students, don't come programmed with perseverance. It is a skill that must be acquired and also endured. But, the result is worth the sweat and tears! Allow your students to have a taste of real personal success.

Did you know?

Perseverance is a personality trait that is associated with being optimistic, positive, and pursuing excellence. http://www.reference.com/motif/education/character-trait-perseverance

Personal Experiences and Stories

In science class we conducted research for constructive and destructive forces. The students were able to choose any topic they desired and were responsible for creating a digital poster board. This allowed for their research to be shared as well as videos and pictures to be added to the virtual poster board (check out discoveryeducation.com and board builder to use this tool). Part of the research required print and digital resources. The students could go to our school website and use DISCUS to have access to thousands of resources from newspapers to journals and encyclopedias. Our librarian was pleased as she showed the students how to maneuver throughout the site. One student actually raised his hand and asked how many clicks he had to make to get the information. Several students commented that it seemed like a lot of clicks on links to get what they needed. They all were visibly put out that it was more than one or two steps to find valuable information! I (Julie) then chimed in the discussion and shared a story about getting one of my graduate degrees and having to use inter-library loans, waiting for books to arrive, using microfiche and microfilm and making copies. The students laughed as I told it and were in shock that I had to go through all of that. They thought it was humorous that I had to wait for something to be delivered to a library and that I had to drive to pick it up. They wanted to see a picture of a machine that used film. One popped up and said that he saw that once in the movies.

After I shared all that I went through, they hesitantly agreed that having to make three or four clicks through different links was a little better than what I had experienced. The students were given sites to explore, including sites with hundreds of videos. I told them to enjoy the journey and not to just focus on getting it done. The journey itself was just as valuable, if not more valuable, then the end result. It gave the end result more meaning. By the time we finished the research project, the students had a taste of what perseverance meant.

When I (Julie) asked my two sons what they had to learn to persevere through during their days in the classroom, this is the list they gave me: projects, exams, reading a novel, listening to a teacher lecture, reading assignments in textbooks, homework assignments, certain classes with specific teachers, classes they didn't enjoy as much, waiting in the never-ending lunch line, standardized tests, and long school days. The list honestly surprised me. My boys love school. They talk about their wonderful teachers and exciting lessons. They brag about their amazing campus and the opportunities they have because they go to such a great school. But to them, the situations listed are a challenge. The situations range from a short period of time to longer stints of time. That tells me that length of time is not directly associated with having to persevere. It also clearly shows that their interest level is directly correlated with their ability to endure the situations. If my boys are interested then they are engaged and more likely to persevere, but if they are not as engaged or interested then it is more of a challenge.

If your students ever complain about things being tough, or about persevering through an assignment, then you might want to share the story of Sir Ernest Shackleton. This is a required reading for my (Brad) class, but for younger students, you could read it to them. Shackleton was a British explorer who led three expeditions to the Antarctic in the early 1900s. His first trip in 1901 was actually under another leader and they traveled to within 745 miles of the South Pole. It was the closest anyone had ever been to the South Pole. In 1917, which was the first expedition he led, Shackleton and his crew got within 97 miles of the South Pole before they had to turn back because they were out of supplies.

In 1914, Shackleton prepared an expedition to sail to Antarctica and then travel across by way of the South Pole. His ship was named the Endurance. He named it after his family motto, which was "By endurance we conquer." Unfortunately the ship became frozen in an ice floe (large pack of floating ice). The crew was stranded and had to abandon ship. The crew had to survive on the floating ice for approximately 14 months until they were finally able to reach an island. Could you imagine the harsh conditions and hopelessness that these men endured to survive such extreme and hopeless conditions for over a year? It kind of puts our problems into perspective. Remarkably not a single person on Shackleton's crew died.

Shackleton, who had no fear of failure, decided the fourth time must be a charm, so in 1922 he planned another expedition to the Antarctic. But as he docked at South Georgia Island preparing for the voyage to the Antarctic, he suffered a heart attack and died. Shackleton never gave up and never feared failure. He attempted some of the most daring expeditions known to man, and he endured all the hardships while keeping his crew safe. His passion to dream big and his perseverance to make his dreams a reality is the reason he is immortalized as one of the greatest explorers in history with many books written and movies made about him.

> **Did you know?**
>
> Building skills like grit and perseverance will help increase college readiness. http://www.deseretnews.com/article/865568540/Experts-say-building-skills-like-grit-and-perseverance-will-help-increase-college-readiness-in-the.html?pg=all

Ideas to Try

Starting with Attitude and Positive Psychology

In order to persevere and cope with failure, we first need to understand the components of a good attitude and tools to think positively.

- **ATTITUDE**: Understanding the components of a great attitude. This can be done in several ways. Here are a few ways that we suggest. (Provided by Dr. Caroline Silby.)

  a. Attitude wheel: Give the students a piece of paper with a blank circle divided into several sections. It should look like a wheel or a pie. As a class, brainstorm a list of words that describe positive attitudes. From that list, the students will choose the ones they want to put in each section of the attitude wheel. When the student exhibits a behavior from a section of the wheel he/she will color in part of the section while also writing the date and a brief explanation on the back of the paper. As the week, month, or semester progresses regularly check the wheel and share the progress of the students in regards to exhibiting characteristics of a great attitude.

  b. Understanding attitude vocabulary: Have students act out, define, and/or discuss the following terms in relation to understanding attitudes. Once students have an understanding of these concepts then they will be able to better apply them.

     ○ Motivated

     ○ Confident

     ○ Open to learning

- Focused
- Happy
- Proud
- Brave
- Aggressive
- Satisfied
- Persistent
- Hard-working
- Positive
- Action-oriented
- Factual
- Non-emotional
- Controlled nerves
- Controlled body

c. Focus board – In art, have the kids create a "Focus Board" to act as a reminder of your ability to create a positive attitude through positive action. You create your own motivational board by writing down the parts of your attitude (i.e. confident, persistent, etc.) that are your strengths or ones you feel like could become your strengths. Then, collect comforting and funny images (photographs, cut-outs from magazines, stickers, drawings, etc.). Post these on the board. You can hang the poster in your locker or they can be posted around homeroom as a way to gain positive energy and connect kids to controllable aspects of performance.

POSITIVE PSYCHOLOGY

1. Take a rubber bracelet and place it on your left wrist. Anytime you worry about something or become negative or down on yourself you must move the bracelet to your right wrist. The goal is to keep the bracelet on your left hand for the entire day, week and eventually the month. Once the bracelet is on your right hand the only way to move it back to the left is to think something positive or take a positive action.

2. Every day for one week, identify three things that you did well. Write them down. Identify and write down one positive action you took

to help achieve that desired result. You will have three actions and three accomplishments.

3. Gratitude: Once a week the students share something they are grateful for in their lives. The first few times students may try to be funny or share very little about themselves but as time goes on the sharing will become deeper and often provide opportunities for deeper group connection. Upon completion of the exercise, have students reflect on how it made them feel to express gratitude.

Tools/Activities to Help Persevere and Learn about Failure

- **Refocus**: Provide students an opportunity during the day to refocus. Use a bell or xylophone and have students stop, breathe, and listen to the sound until it stops. This allows them to quietly reconnect to the present moment. It can be used to initiate discussion about the benefits of refocusing in the classroom. It can be used if students feel overwhelmed and need a break. This is a tool that can allow them to be able to persevere.

- **Teach self-talk**: What does perseverance sound like or feel like inside? It's often hard to recognize and even harder to develop without coaching. What phrases resonate for you? For your child? How about: "I can make this work!", "Don't give up!", "I am blessed!", or even "Challenges are made to overcome!" This helps students when they have failed in an activity to overcome the failure and look forward to the next task. It helps them realize something positive about themselves and gives them confidence to continue on.

- **Goal setting**: The key here is to develop some attainable goals. Discuss the difference between short- and long-term goals. Give examples of each and then let students set and track their goal progress. Discuss when goals are not reached. What happens then? Do they fail and do they quit? Do they make different goals? Goal setting helps students continue to progress and reevaluate often. This can help with experiencing success and failure and learning how to cope with each situation.

- **Read a book about a leader** who persevered through many difficulties. Some of these individuals include Lee Iacocca, Margaret Thatcher, William Wilberforce, and Ernest Shackleton. This is usually an activity for older students, but can be used at any level as long as the students can connect with the person.

- **Create a calendar or long-term planning tool**: When an assignment or activity expands over a longer period of time it is easy for students to lose interest or get distracted. Help them prepare a plan to stay on task for the time needed. Create checkpoints so that you as a teacher are involved and aware if the students are on task.

- **Challenge excellence in the classroom**: Real growth happens when people work at the edge of their competence. Students who are not challenged lose out on the sense of confidence that comes from mastering a challenge, and they may come to believe that accomplishment should be effortless. Challenging means that failure is possible. Bring students to that level. Let them fail. Allow students to rework certain assignments. This helps students understand that work can be improved and that mastery should be a goal when working as well.

- **Encourage effort and practice, more than accomplishment**: Many students worry that they aren't good enough, which makes them give up easily. Help them understand that no one becomes accomplished overnight. All experts have worked for years to accomplish excellence in their field. Reinforce the idea that perseverance more than any other trait is often most associated with success. This is a wonderful discussion topic when connecting to the professions students are interested in when they are in the real world. How are they going to get there? What is the plan? How long will it take? This gives them a personal connection with effort and practice equaling accomplishment.

Key Points to Remember

- Teaching short-term and long-term goal setting is important.
- Remember that attitude is everything! Having a positive attitude and working on skills to keep attitude optimal are a critical piece of dealing with failure or overcoming obstacles.
- Provide strategies for dealing with stress and failing with the first few attempts.
- Help them with organization and planning skills.
- Model putting forth good effort.

- Share stories (personal or within pop-culture) of success and failure with positive or negative work ethics.

- Positive self-talk. Redirect students' self-defeating language – focus on can, not can't.

- Focus on achieving progress – not simply the end result (enjoy the journey!).

- Allow students the opportunity to fail; otherwise they will never appreciate success.

- Celebrate accomplishments! (We have publishing parties in our writer's workshop classes.)

- Create scenarios where students find solutions to problems, thereby improving their decision-making skills.

- Make the connection between practice and perseverance/failure, so students see it as part of the process and not as a dead end.

11 | Don't Childproof Education

> *" We spend the first twelve months of our children's lives teaching them to walk and talk and the next twelve telling them to sit down and shut up. "*
>
> Phyllis Diller

Our Thoughts and Some Research Too

Learning is an important characteristic of human behavior. Think of how babies crawl on the floor looking for objects, which then go directly into their mouths. At first glance you would think the baby is hungry, or, as Freud thought, there is an oral fixation. In reality, the baby is actively exploring and learning. Their learning is active and experiential. When learning, babies naturally use all of their senses.

However, adults often hamper this inquisitive nature of children. What is the first thing a young couple does when having a baby? They "baby proof" their homes. Basically, they want the child to sit still in one place all day, so he doesn't harm himself. While part of this behavior is a concern for safety (we get that and even encourage it!), it may also be that the parents don't want the extra work that is required to keep up with the young child. We understand that having a child is hard work, especially once they start to crawl and walk. But that doesn't mean they should be put in a protective bubble.

Children naturally want to explore, play, and be creative. They tend to live within the moment and can make anything magical. They live without a fear of failure or being harmed. They will climb, jump, and play without a care in the world. It is refreshing. I have often said that if we could bottle up the energy of a child and sell it then we would be rich.

Where does that energy go? Where is the carefree attitude? Where is the desire to explore and play? Does age affect that mentality? Does society? Can teenagers act this way? What about adults? When is the last time you have been to an amusement park? Did you have just a brief sense of that joy and carefree feeling? Adults have brief stints of feeling like a child, but due to responsibility, pressure, and what some would say, real-life, they do not experience it enough.

How can we as teachers allow students to still be children? Have the school systems childproofed education? Unfortunately, the answer leans more towards yes than no. Teachers lecture and students listen. Teachers cram in information to prepare for exams and standardized tests. There are many educators who would prefer that students sit at desks and work quietly and count that as a successful day, regardless of whether or not the student actually learned anything. This description may require little effort, but is this really education? Then we wonder why students don't enjoy learning. Students spend on average seven hours in school and then are often expected to work another one or two at home on homework. Does that sound like fun? It sounds like an assembly-line model. It sounds like hours of busy work. Where is the joy in that?

Standardized tests and exams are the main reason that education is being childproofed. We are not bashing standardized tests or the need for taking exams. There are pros and cons to administering standardized tests and giving exams, but the key aspect is to *not teach to the test*. It is essential for the school to know why they are giving the tests. Too often schools are worried about the passing rate (and the funding connected to it) and feel that drilling the students with information will help them to better succeed. This is simply not true. Children enter school with enthusiasm and a sense of wonder, which can enhance their desire to learn and excel. They naturally learn through exploration, play, creativity, and yes, even hard work. But too often these traits are not reinforced because they aren't thought to be necessary to pass a standardized test. We must remember that children learn through many mediums, which can actually involve playing and having fun. Even brain-based research suggests that learning is enhanced when children are moving and active.

Have you ever wondered why children start school with "wide-eyed wonder" and excitement, but typically by fourth grade, school has become a boring routine? As prominent psychiatrist Dr. Stuart Brown states, "Teachers feel like they're under huge pressures to get academic excellence to the exclusion of having much fun in the classroom. But playful learning leads to better academic success than the skills-and-drills approach." Could you imagine having a classroom where students come in every day and retain their wide-eyed sense of wonder and excitement? This description of behavior is a far cry from many classrooms where students are expected to sit still and memorize fragmented bits of information. What a contradiction to their inquisitive and exploring nature.

For many teachers this type of teaching calls for a paradigm shift. Giving up some control of the classroom to allow for play and exploration can be a scary and challenging task. Will the students learn? Will they perform well on tests? Will they meet all of the curriculum standards? This is where designing meaningful lessons is critical. I (Julie) often ask my students more questions than giving them answers. They ask me a question and I ask them another right back. For example, I had a student ask me if swinging was an example of Newton's third law. I asked that student what he thought and if he could also make a connection to any other of Newton's Laws. When I do this to students they don't get mad. Their eyes light up because I have given them another challenge to explore. That natural inquisitive behavior shines. That student ran to the swings, hopped on, and then yelled back to me that it is also inertia and then promptly explained how. So while a paradigm shift may be hard, it is not only necessary but worth it!

Make learning engaging and, yes, fun. Learning can be enjoyable and satisfying even when it requires work. Much like your job, learning is hard work, but at the end of the day the work produces a sense of satisfaction. Remember as adults we try new activities that we find fun, engaging, or of value to us. We don't typically participate in activities that we don't like or find useful to our lives. Why do we expect children to be any different? I have always taught using the philosophy that when I think teaching is a job then I need to quit. That sums it up for me. To me a job is monotonous and boring. My classroom is far from that. If I get bored talking in front of the class then it means I have talked too long. There is a good chance the students are also bored. I like to conduct experiments and learn by doing. I am still inquisitive by nature. I look through the lens of the students and design my lessons with their interests in mind. Students often feel like they are playing and at times are amazed by how much they learn. It is safe to say that while my class is fun and engaging, it also is one of the most challenging that they have. This is because they have to think, be inquisitive, explore, discover, and find out the answers. I refuse to spoon feed them information.

Children are also very social beings that need to develop their interpersonal skills. They naturally do this through play. These skills are all but ignored in education today and yet we continue to wonder why students are disrespectful, act like bullies, and can have a hard time developing healthy relationships with teachers and peers. Ultimately the skills that are required for today's culture include respect, responsibility, and the building of intentional relationships. Part of the challenge of instilling these skills in today's classroom is that we want the "quick fix," and there is no "quick remedy" for some concerns. The students have to be given time to work within groups or teams and to interact with peers. This type of work will model play and allow them the chance to build these interpersonal skills.

Another aspect of developing interpersonal skills requires the students have time to actually interact socially. Unfortunately, opportunities such as recess are distant memories in many school systems. Why? So we can make more time for testing or more lessons on how to read? Some schools take recess time away for bad behavior. Students get to sit on a bench for ten minutes and watch their friends play. A major research study showed that children with more than fifteen minutes of recess a day showed better behavior in class than those who had little or none. Regrettably, this study also revealed that children exposed to none or minimal recess were much more likely to be black, to be from families with lower incomes and lower levels of education, to live in large cities, and to be from the Northeast or South. Why do these school systems take recess or playtime away from students? Don't they realize that they are childproofing education?

Remember students instinctively want to discover and learn, so let's provide them the opportunity to succeed, not simply on a test, but in life. Remember the old adage, "Work hard and play hard." Let's do both in the classroom.

Did you know?

Fun is a perspective. If you are not having fun, then you are not doing it right! http://tinybuddha.com/blog/how-to-have-fun-like-children-15-joyful-tips

Personal Experiences and Stories

I (Brad) remember asking a young child once if he enjoyed school. He replied that his teacher had too many rules. He said it was too hard to remember them all but real easy to break them. I laughed at the response, but it did give insight into his perception of school. He saw school as a bunch of rules to follow, rather than a fun and engaging place to learn. When I have asked most students why they go to school, do you know what their reply is? Most often it is to see their friends. So why do schools seem to want to limit this social interaction? Schools should create opportunities to affirm this type of socialization on their campuses. Class time can be, in a more open, active, collaborative, project-based environment, far more social than it has been in the past. Schools can also affirm students socializing in the length of breaks they provide during lunch and between periods and by making fun and social interactions part of the daily norm. Schools where children are not growing socially or enjoying learning have childproofed the educational process.

So, do you know if you childproof your classroom? I (Julie) gave our faculty a chance to reflect by the use of a song. One year we started off a faculty meeting with me playing the song *"Flowers are Red"* by Harry Chapin. We listened to the entire song without interruption. (If you have not listened to it, you should put this book down and play it. It will change your view of education for life.) Then we sat silently for about a minute and reflected. Finally I led a wonderful discussion asking the teachers to share feelings that they felt as the song went on. One teacher in the room said she saw herself as the teacher in the song and was shocked by how she would be perceived by the students. She has often told students the colors to use and what and when to paint. She also has removed students for not following directions. This is a caring teacher, not a tyrant. But she shared that she never thought of it from the child's point of view. She has taught for over 20 years and it took one song at the beginning of a faculty meeting to change how she will run her classroom. She realized she was taking the joy and fun out of her classroom. I suggest playing the song to your faculty. It is powerful.

Do boys and girls react differently when given the chance to play and explore in the classroom? Absolutely. I (Julie) have had the opportunity to listen to many speakers who specialize in gender learning differences. Every single one of them stresses that the genders are different and that you need a classroom that will accommodate all types of learners. Let boys stand at their seats. Let them draw pictures of war or write about things that are more violent. It is OK as long as they stay within the parameters that are set. Girls on the other hand have better fine motor skills in their pre-puberty age. Girls tend to be better at the verbal aspects at a younger age while boys perform better on visual–spatial activities and physical activities. Keeping these things in mind while setting up an active classroom is vital to classroom management.

I personally do not have many discipline issues because I respect these gender differences and allow standing when needed or moving around by the students. My classroom is designed to allow for learning experiences; it is definitely not childproofed and restrictive!

Do we give standardized tests at our school? Yes. Our school just went through that analysis and we decided that it was one assessment among many to give us a complete picture of the students' abilities. We recognize that it is one test given on a specific day and that it can't be the only major assessment used to measure ability. Our students have writing portfolios, we administer other types of assessments frequently throughout the year, and we have detailed checklists for skills for each student. We are not allowing standardized tests to childproof education in our school.

Did you know?

Playing enhances creativity and promotes critical thinking skills. http://www.naeyc.org/tyc/files/tyc/file/V4N5/Tools%20to%20Enhance%20Young%20CHildren%27s%20Thinking.pdf

Ideas to Try

How to NOT Childproof Your Classroom!

- Be willing to allow for an active classroom. This may include noise and movement!
- Be willing to give up some control and let students lead some learning concepts.
- Allow students to discover answers and not always give them the answer. This means they have to learn how to fail and then solve the problem on their own!
- Give time for exploration! Actually put this in your lesson plan book!
- Use cooperative learning strategies within your teaching.
- Allow group work or partner work (peer reading is an excellent way to bring this into literature/reading classes).

- Teach students movements to go along with lessons. (In reader's workshop there are hand signals to use every time a student hears a certain word. These hand signals are used in every subject area, not just reading.)

- Sing and dance when possible. (In science class we create a cell song or cell rap as a quiz grade to assess vocabulary comprehension. Students may use musical instruments or music and are required to have movement.)

- Create learning stations

  - In science class we have station labs where students move around and participate in different activities at each lab table.

  - In writer's workshop students have various stations such as a publishing station, an editing station, and a private work station.

- Have classroom management expectations established and clearly posted.

  - All students can have ownership in this process by brainstorming together. Let them help with designing the rules and they are more likely to adhere to them.

  - Be sure to have logical consequences if someone does not follow a rule. (If a student does not follow lab rules then the student only observes and does not actively participate in the lab. They don't lose recess time. The consequence must match the behavior.)

  - Students can create the posters or signs for the management plan.

  - Students can also sign a management contract that they helped design.

- Make sure noise level and expectations are clear for every student for each activity.

  - Be sure to explain the activity and then make a connection with the behavioral expectations. We cannot assume the students will know this. We have signs posted with numbers that correlate with noise levels. These are done throughout our entire lower school, so students recognize them whenever they are in any part of campus.

- Implement both teamwork and cooperative learning opportunities.

  - Jigsaw activities can be used in any subject area.

  - Cooperative learning resource books and resource materials are abundant. I recommend any of the Tribes Learning Community books by Jeanne Gibbs. We have several sets of these in our school and guidance office.

- Allow for technology to be integrated within the classrooms. Podcasting, videos, and songs allow creativity to flow!

- Have art supplies available for students to use at any time. The students should feel that the classroom is their space and not that they should have to ask permission to use everything. (I have an area that has crayons, glue sticks, markers, extra pencils, staplers, hole punchers, cap erasers, tape, paper, etc. The students know they can use the materials at any time.)

Key Points to Remember

- Remember these are **children** within your classroom.

- Create a safe environment where students feel they can explore, fail, and succeed.

- Allow for creativity within the classroom. Bring in the arts whenever possible.

- Make teamwork and group work an essential aspect within your classroom to allow for social growth.

- Give up some control and allow for student-guided, creative, personalized, meaningful educational experiences.

- Students need to feel like they can still be children. Allow play within the classroom and give unstructured time to interact and move around.

- For older children, give them time to socialize with each other as well, like an extended lunch break outside or take a recess break once a week. Even a walk around the track will be a refreshing break from sitting at desks all day.

12 | Instill Vigor

" Enthusiasm is the mother of effort, and without it nothing great was ever achieved. "

Ralph Waldo Emerson

Our Thoughts and Some Research Too

One of the main concepts of the book is to find what talents students possess and develop those talents so that they will be more successful in life. Whether we view these as talents, strengths, or even our life purpose, everyone has potential that needs to be unleashed. But can this potential be unleashed in a very restrictive and controlled environment?

Have you ever met someone who seemed to be invigorated by life? Have you ever seen someone like Tony Robbins give a motivational speech? It makes you want to jump up and change your life immediately. Maybe a coach giving an inspiring pregame speech, or even a fitness instructor who has such enthusiasm that you make sure that you fit her class into your busy schedule. These people invigorate us. They make us feel energized and alive. Whenever we speak or do workshops, we make sure that the energy in the room is palpable because enthusiasm is contagious!

One of the buzzwords in education over the past few years has been rigor. It appears that rather than focusing on energizing students, the focus is on making education more rigorous so that our test scores are compatible with other countries. But what is rigor? Rigor is defined by Webster as: harsh inflexibility in opinion, temper, or judgment: the quality of being unyielding or inflexible: an act or instance of strictness, severity, or cruelty: a condition that makes life difficult, challenging, or uncomfortable. Rigor mortis is actually a term associated with death. This doesn't sound like a term associated with enthusiasm and unleashing potential.

Since standardized testing has done little to improve education, I would say education has definitely met the criteria for rigor mortis. Rigor may well be the most defining characteristic of a slowly dying educational system. This is not to say that education should not be challenging, difficult, or require hard work. However, when education is strict, rigid, and inflexible in opinion and judgment, then it is not committed to meeting the needs of students, but rather having students conform to its goals.

Rigor has created a very isolating educational environment. Students must act within a rigid set of behaviors – seated quietly, not allowed to move freely from place to place, and walk in a straight line. Students are learning the same content at the same rate in which learning is typically confined to the classroom and more specifically the desk. Children are conditioned to prevent themselves from squirming. Free time or recess has all but been eliminated from some classrooms.

Ironically, most teachers were successful students, who did sit quietly at their desk, completed their work, and succeeded in an inflexible, rigid learning environment. But, they are in the minority of students who did successfully complete a college education. While most teachers succeeded in such an environment, it is clear that it may be counter productive to many students. Maybe rigor is not what is needed in education today after all.

Education today needs to be more adaptive and fluid rather than rigid and inflexible. The term that best fits this type of education would be vigorous. Vigor means having intensity, energy, and enthusiasm. It is the potential for enhancing "active strength of body or mind." When something is in**vigor**ating, it is "stimulating . . . energizing . . . restorative." Even if it's a difficult task, at the end of the experience you feel empowered and ready to try again. Vigor trains students to work hard and at a high level of excellence for maximum achievement.

Students should be full of enthusiasm when it comes to many areas of their lives and education should be one of them. As adults there are many aspects of our lives where we should feel invigorated, such as relationships, careers, helping others, and even with our health. When is the last time you felt invigorated about something? Did you take a group fitness class after a long day of teaching only to feel more energized than before you went to the class? Maybe you went to a workshop and learned a concept for the class that you can't wait to try out. Hopefully reading this book has invigorated you.

What would vigor look like in a classroom? Vigor in education is likely to be driven by internal motivation, passion, guidance, and mentoring. The delivery method is likely to be diverse and adaptable to the interests and real-world experiences of the students. Collaboration and cooperative learning would complement individualized assessments. While the classroom can be systematic and deliberate, it is also flexible to the needs of the students. The level of content being covered is not diminished. It is just the opposite. The level of content can be as challenging as need be; it is just presented in a way that motivates the students and helps them to experience passion through mentoring and guidance. Learning should be individualized whenever possible. Again, it doesn't mean that the students all have their own learning plan. But maybe there are learning paths, options for students to have within the objectives that need to be covered. Remember, as teachers we are literally vying for the attention of students. Living immersed in a highly stimulating environment has taken its toll on the adolescent learner.

The effective teacher embraces vigor as the intersection between the challenge of the task and the interest of the student. This creates an invigorating learning experience for all students. Help students find their drive, connect it to the classroom and the desire to succeed will be apparent. The world of academe will actually become more challenging and more complex as a result of the students being actively engaged in their own learning process. The challenging tasks are part of the high expectations you set for students. Students will typically rise to the high expectations you set for them if you have developed a good rapport with them. The importance of this connection is that students will face high expectations in many aspects of life and need to be prepared to handle them. Whether it is the ball field, performing in a band, or trying to reach sales goals, there will always be a need for hard work to succeed.

What does a school look like that focuses on vigor? Class or course offerings would need to be varied with not every student following the same curricular path. This means starting at the elementary level. Are the Arts and Languages recognized along with the core courses? Many students obtain jobs in those areas while our schools tend to focus only on the core courses (math, reading, science, history). A perfect example of this is computer science. It is one of the most lucrative and fastest growing professions in the world, but is it even acknowledged in most schools? Knowing that not all students want to attend college, the schools would need to offer other options for the students. What about offering trade school courses or having a connection within the community for job shadowing? Are there counselors or advisees who can help the students plan their own path? Is there support for parents to help them become aware of options for their children? Schools focusing on challenging the students while recognizing their passion would successfully prepare the student for the real world upon graduation.

Vigor, much like all of the skills that have been discussed throughout the book, is not easily measured on a standardized test, yet it is critical in determining how successful and happy a person will be in his career, family, and life in general. Unlocking the passion of a student is the ultimate goal of education. Remember, as Williams Butler Yeats once said, "Education is not the filling of a pail, but the lighting of a fire." The question then becomes are you a bucket filler or a fire lighter? The bucket is limiting, rigid, and can only hold a limited amount of information. However, lighting a fire has unlimited potential and can grow in size and intensity. Therefore, ignite the passion in your students so they can reach their full potential.

Did you know?

Having passion is the formula for limitless curiosity. http://www.ted.com/conversations/18629/education_is_not_about_school.html

Personal Experiences and Stories

While learning can be fun and entertaining at times, as we discussed in the edutainment section, there are times when learning should be hard work. It is like the feeling you get after a hard workout in the gym. During the workout, it is not always fun or easy, but you know it is helping you achieve a goal; it is not simply wasting your time. Education often feels more like a waste of time to students. Work must be good for students; they should see that it is beneficial to them. For example, besides teaching, I (Brad) have also coached as I mentioned earlier. I remember one student who tried out for my basketball team several years ago. I actually had a couple of teachers who told me that I didn't want him on my team because he was a discipline problem in class. He was described to me as the bad apple that would spoil the whole bushel. But, fortunately, I had another teacher who said that if he was good enough to make the team it would be beneficial for him to be a part of a team. She knew his home life wasn't great and it seemed like he could use a break.

Well, he actually did a good job at tryouts, so I kept him on the team. He was so excited to be a part of the team. He worked hard, was never late for practice, and got better with every practice. As I mentioned before, I also work on life skills with student athletes such as attitude, leadership, goal setting, and work ethic. Within just a couple of weeks, every one of his teachers either stopped by in person or emailed me to let me know how much he had improved in class. He was no longer a discipline problem, but worked very hard in class. His grades were improving and by the middle of the season, he had earned a starting position. It was amazing to see the transformation of this young man over the course of the basketball season. He found something he enjoyed and worked hard to excel at it, and it changed other aspects of his life as well.

Now, let's take this same concept and implement it into our schools. First, we need to offer a variety of opportunities for students to find and share their passion. On the first day of class, I would have students share their interests, hobbies, and extracurricular activities. I would keep a file of these activities and during the course of the year, I would find ways to link different activities to the classroom. I remember one student in class who wasn't one of the smartest students, but he loved the outdoors. He loved fishing, hunting, and knew a lot about the plants and trees in the area. So, rather than teach topics like plants, or identifying tress with a PowerPoint or lecture, I would take the students into the woods and let this student teach the class about certain trees. I had no problem admitting that the student knew as much as me (maybe more) about the trees and plants. When students are given the opportunity to show you and others what they know, I have seen faces literally light up with pride and passion.

I (Brad) know of several childcare programs in Canada and in Europe where students are outside all day long. One daycare director said there is no such thing as poor weather, just poor clothing choices. While I don't know if I would enjoy the outdoors for hours at a time anymore, as a child I would have loved this program because I spent most of my waking hours outdoors anyway. One of the first in Canada opened its doors, or rather its gates about six years ago. The Carp Ridge Forest Pre-School offers its students few comforts like toys, climate control, or electric power in Ottawa's rural western outskirts. Instead, it boasts a garden, trails through the woods, and a tent-like shelter called a yurt, and aims to help children aged three to six connect with nature. In the UK and throughout Europe these are known as forest kindergartens. While this may conjure up images of Hansel and Gretel, the students do much more than walk around the woods all day. Because the activities are not manufactured by toys, prefab games, or other

What Schools Don't Teach

curriculum, students are involved in more authentic learning. Many of the noted benefits of this vigorous program include improved skills such as: constructive contributions to learning, asking questions and interest in learning, motivation, sports, music, art and creativity, and even positive social behavior. Imagine if we moved beyond the walls of the classroom and brought the passion and invigoration of the real world back to learning.

Many students may find it hard to get enthusiastic about school if the sole focus is on standardized testing. However, if the students can participate in activities which interest them then they are much more likely to work hard. If students learn to work hard and feel the satisfaction from hard work, and understand that it is important and valuable, then they will continue to work hard.

It is similar to working out at a health club. How many people do you know who say they either don't have time to work out, or they don't have the energy at the end of the day to workout. I (Brad) have worked with adults in the past who used these as excuses. However, once I convinced them to stick with a program for three weeks, it was amazing to see the change in their intensity and enthusiasm to training. First, I had to find activities that they would actually do for three weeks and then make sure they were successful in achieving goals. By the end of three weeks, most people have more energy at the end of the day, experience some weight loss, and feel an overall sense of improved fitness. They feel invigorated and want to continue. With these people, just as with students, it's not that they aren't willing to work hard, but sometimes they have to have a well-developed plan to get them to that point. Then success breeds success and the students feel energized to try more and take more risks!

Did you know?

Eighty percent of employees are unhappy with their jobs. People who work within their passion are more satisfied. http://www.businessinsider. com/what-do-you-do-when-you-hate-your-job-2010-10

Ideas to Try

- **Get to know your students**: Take time to get to know your students to find out what they are truly passionate about. Give them interest inventories, let them share, talk with them, listen to them, allow journaling.

114

Use any technique in which you are comfortable to get to know your students beyond who has what grade in your subject area.

- **Allow student input**: While it's important for the teacher to keep students on task and motivated, allowing them to have some choice and control over what happens in the classroom is a great way to keep them engaged. For example, give them a voice on class rules and consequences. Allow students to vote whenever possible. This gives them buy-in and makes them feel valued. Students who are in an environment where they feel valued and safe will be more likely to open up and share their passions.

- **Enthusiasm is contagious**: Let students see what invigorates you about school. If you teach science, teach it in such a way that you make it their favorite subject. I (Julie) love teaching science and my students know it. I model being enthusiastic and energetic. That energy is contagious. Year after year I have students and parents tell me that science is their favorite subject because of how it is taught.

- **Intrinsic desire**: Help students find their own reasons for doing class work and working hard. It can be because they find the material interesting, want to go to college, or just love to learn, it is one of the most powerful tools you can give them. Recognizing these interests is essential in being able to set goals and follow passions.

- **Personalized projects and activities**: Remember education is personal and one of the best ways to get students invigorated about education is to make it personal to their lives. Let them research a topic in which they are interested. It can be sports, music, outdoors, cartoons, video games, or even something as simple as Legos. Let them read a book of their choice. Let them work with students of their choice. Making a project or activity personalized will give them the opportunity to choose a topic about which they are passionate.

- **Showcase talents**: Give students the opportunity to shine! This will help validate their passion and share their accomplishments. It will also help them gain confidence and recognize their hard work and effort.

- **Create an environment to promote passion**: Why read at a desk when you can read in a loft or on pillows on the floor? Why color a poster board when you can generate an interactive board with video and sound that you can show through Apple TV to the whole class? Take a look at your classroom space. Does it promote passion? Is the students' work hanging on the walls? Is it colorful and inviting? Even with the smallest of budgets a room can be converted from a classroom to a learning environment. The environment sets the stage for the learning to begin!

- **Drop everything and play**: Remember the drop everything and read initiative? Well I always incorporated a drop everything and play. Remember the motto, Work Hard and Play Hard? Well I made sure my students understood this as more than just a quote. I got the idea from coaching youth football many years ago. The head coach would call off practice every few weeks and would make the practice time a study hall, where we actually worked with the students on schoolwork, or occasionally he would make it a play day. We would bring water balloons, shaving cream, bring food, and have a party instead of practice. The athletes loved it and it proved to be a great break to reinvigorate them. So, once every few weeks I would take my class and either play a game, or simply make it a study hall where they could work in groups on classwork or another subject in which they needed help. The students loved this "break" from the rigor of academics and it really did seem to reinvigorate them!

- **Design a new course**: Our registrar often gives a heavy sigh when we create new courses. She says we keep adding, but never take any away. Well, that is because we keep seeing the need for new classes to meet the needs of our students. I love that one teacher in our science department is now offering a bird watching course. It is his passion and he is sharing it with the students. He does teach the required science courses, but offers an elective course on bird watching. Our school has also continued to offer higher-level Chinese, Latin, and Art courses because of the desire shown by the students.

Key Points to Remember

- Provide options where students can give input into lessons and the learning process. A feeling of connection and ownership will increase student motivation. Let them show off their interests and expertise to the class.

- Improve teaching and curricula to make school more relevant and engaging and enhance the connection between school and the real world.

- Improve instruction and access to supports for struggling students, so they don't feel left behind.

- Build a school climate that fosters the essential Rs (respect, responsibility, relationships, and relevance).

- Create a culture of high expectations and an emphasis on vigor in the learning process. This can't be said enough, but instill within the students the ethics of work hard and play hard.

- Allow fluid movement within the classroom. Students should not be confined to desks.

- Create a reading or writing center, including a publishing center or presentation center. (We had lofts built in our first grade classrooms to have special reading areas for students.)

- Create an inviting learning environment, including the display of student work in classrooms and hallways. Create products of use, not just something that is tossed in the garbage can the next day.

13 | **Model Flexibility**

" The measure of intelligence is the ability to change."

Albert Einstein

Our Thoughts and Some Research Too

How much flexibility do students have in school? We're not talking about their ability to touch their toes, which we haven't been able to do in a while, but their ability to adapt. Much like leadership, students aren't provided very many opportunities to develop or flex their flexibility muscles. You have to look no further than the past two decades and the technology explosion to see the importance of flexibility and adapting to change. About the only thing that has remained the same is our school systems. However, if students are going to succeed in school, college, and life beyond school, they need to learn to adapt and be flexible.

Flexibility is a skill that focuses on a child's ability to adapt to new situations, improvise, and shift strategies to meet different types of challenges. This skill is highly valued in the business world and most leadership models suggest that it is a key trait of effective leadership. The world today is about more than just being flexible in regards to switching a career; it is being flexible in daily situations in regards to emotional ability to lead peers in collaborative groups. While being flexible is not a new concept, it is more paramount in today's global economy because of the fast paced changes occurring with technology and society.

It often seems that students simply follow each other class to class all day like going through an assembly line, but is that truly the case? While there have to be rules, structure, and consequences in school, a rigid and inflexible environment is not the ideal setting to maximize student growth. The students often walk in straight lines, have assigned seats, all follow one set of directions, and are all on the same daily schedule. This is how it appears from the outside, but their daily lives are a little more complex than that. Students interact with one another and with teachers. They are hopefully in classes where there are projects, cooperative learning, teamwork, differentiated instruction, presentations, and more occurring. Students have numerous situations occurring where they need to be flexible. It may be as simple as wanting to choose a book for a project, but someone else has already chosen that book. What do they do? How do they react? Do they cry and demand the book or do they choose another book? What if a student is late to school and misses a class? What if their regular seat is taken? What if they get put in a group with people they do not like? What if there is nothing they like to eat for lunch? What if materials are left at home? What if they wore the wrong uniform requirements for that day? What if a friend is playing with someone else at recess? What if they have to make up a quiz, but also have other work they need to do? What if their parents are late to pick them up? Flexibility is a factor that needs to be recognized, addressed, and focused on within our schools in order to help students experience success and grow as individuals.

The scenarios are limitless with issues that students face daily and to them these are real and important situations. How they react to these everyday situations shows if they understand what being flexible means. Do they know how to problem-solve? Do students understand how to make a new plan, navigate through that plan and re-evaluate the situation? Do they know when to let emotions get involved? Do they know when to ask for help? These are all traits or aspects of flexibility. Are these being taught within your class?

Do students have the opportunity to work through all of these stages or aspects in order to make decisions when a change has to occur? It is essential that we are focusing on their real-life situations and helping students to experience success in regards to being flexible. Only after the students have learned to be flexible in their own life will they be able to transfer that to the real world later on in life. Even with testing, students need to be flexible and be able to adapt. For example, when taking a test that contains both multiple choice and essay questions, a child with good flexibility will be able to switch easily between the various formats, while a child who struggles with flexibility may get stuck and become frustrated.

There is not a profession that doesn't require flexibility. Being flexible is a trait that employers value. America's Job Exchange shares that employers and fellow employees value flexibility. Being flexible will make for a healthier work environment and a healthier life. Boston College conducted a study sharing that more families now have two parents working full time than ever before in history. This has made the employers become flexible with scheduling to where employees, if possible, can work from different locations, including home, if it better suits the family. This type of flexibility has actually increased productivity and made for a healthier work environment.

The United States is not the only country that values flexibility. According to The University of Kent (The UK's European university), "The world of work is changing at an ever increasing pace so employers actively seek out graduates who can adapt to changing circumstances and environments, and embrace new ideas, who are enterprising, resourceful and adaptable." Major companies like IBM describe the flexible workplace as "a virtualized and physical environment characterized by connections, collaboration, and user choice that enables the worker to be more agile and perform activities anywhere, anytime." It is obvious that flexibility is a valued trait and one that students must learn in order to fit in and experience success in our ever-changing world.

Did you know?

Flexibility is considered one of the main traits of effective leadership.
http://www.fastcompany.com/3004914/5-characteristics-great-leaders

Personal Experiences and Stories

Once when I (Julie) was interviewing for a job I had to teach a sample lesson. In the middle of passing out materials to model food chains, the fire alarm went off. I had spent hours planning the "perfect lesson" that was sure to "wow" the principal and students. Instead, I calmly instructed the students to leave the materials on their tables and line up at the door. We walked outside and spent the next 15 minutes performing the fire drill. By the time we returned in class I had about 20 minutes to teach a 50-minute lesson. I explained to the students the plan for the lesson and together we came up with a way to modify the lesson and still be able to perform the activity. It was not exactly what I planned, but it ended up being successful because I was willing to be flexible and modify the lesson. The principal was stunned that I didn't want to schedule another day of teaching since my time had been cut short. She was amazed at how the students and I together made the lesson work. She said that not only did I teach about food chains, but I also taught a life lesson to the students about being able to modify and adjust in a situation. Needless to say, I was offered the job.

I could not honestly get through a day if I didn't know how to be flexible. I would say that this is one of the most important and often challenging aspects of my job. I teach science, but I also am the LS curriculum coordinator, which means at various times of the day I have different duties and responsibilities. I may have a student at my door needing help studying the bones of the frog at the same time that I am expected to be in a meeting about redesigning our media center. There are times when I have to be in a meeting or should be grading papers while my own children are playing a tennis match or a baseball game. Prioritizing and being flexible are the only way that I get through my day. Sometimes I just have to let some things go and know I will get to it later. I cannot allow myself to feel like I have failed because I quickly remind myself of what I have already accomplished. I make a new plan and continue on my way towards the next task. When I begin to feel overwhelmed I know I need a break. These are all self-taught attributes. That is one reason I feel that knowing how to be flexible is such an important aspect to teach our students. If they can be flexible and prioritize and be able to make changes then they will be better prepared for the real world. There have been times when I was immersed in situations where I had to learn to be flexible. I did not always handle all of those situations very well and wish I had the tools that I do now.

As mentioned earlier, flexibility means to adapt to new situations, improvise, and shift strategies to meet different types of challenges. In a global world, flexibility takes on a new perspective when it comes to dealing with other cultures as well. This was made clear to me when I (Brad) had the opportunity to travel to Malaysia to help develop a teaching certification for their teachers.

While traveling through the country, most people couldn't speak English very well. However I did have a translator who helped me in conversations and even taught me some phrases, so they loved it when I spoke in their native tongue. While there, I had to stay in a teaching dormitory where toilet paper and air-conditioning were almost non-existent. Fortunately, my translator let me know what to expect, so before leaving a major city, I stocked up on toilet paper and Dr. Pepper for the trip out to the country.

I also had to adapt to some of the cultural taboos, such as putting your foot on a chair, or pointing with your finger, which are both considered rude in their culture. I remember a specific moment while talking in class that I propped my foot up on a chair, which I always did as a science teacher. When I saw several eyes bug out of their heads, I realized I had done something improper. Fortunately, I shared with them that I might be ignorant of some of their customs and I hoped they would forgive me and let me know when I mess up. With all eyes on me, I quickly took my foot off of the chair and continued the discussion. I did return home pointing with my thumb instead of my index finger, which my family thought was strange.

I could have been nervous about visiting a very different culture, but I was willing to be flexible and adapt to their world. Fortunately, I am not a picky eater, so I got to try some exotic dishes and delicacies such as durian and rambutans. Some tasted great and some were not that tasty. It was an experience that I will never forget and would have never experienced it if I had not been willing to travel to the other side of the world and adapt to their culture.

Did you know?

Flexibility increases student involvement, which is directly correlated with academic success. www.decd.sa.gov.au/limestonecoast/files/pages/new%20page/PLC/teachers_make_a_difference.pdf

Ideas to Try

- **Model flexibility**: Acknowledge times when you have to be flexible in your profession. When appropriate, share these with your students so they can see how you handle having to be flexible.

- **Teach tools and traits needed to be flexible**: Identify tools or traits needed to be flexible. Just by having the students recognize these traits will help them eventually learn how to use them. Traits include such things as patience, problem solving, listening, list making, setting goals, prioritizing, compromise, organization, and collaboration.

- **Students practice flexibility to help you**: Let the students help you to solve a problem that may occur during class. Not only will this model that you are willing to be flexible, but it also models that you value them and trust them to help be a part of the solution. You may have to give them guidelines the first few times. Usually a solution occurs after brainstorming options, discussing the options by using pros and cons, choosing a plan, and then executing that plan. The final and often forgotten stage is reflection. It is essential that you give the students time to reflect on their plan and decide if the plan worked as they thought.

- **Give students problem situations to simulate them having to be flexible**: These situations can be used for guidance lessons or for building classroom relationships. If it is a guidance lesson then the topic usually stems around friendship or social issues. Being flexible in those situations will help to foster healthier relationships. We have modeled situations such as someone picking the same book you want to read or someone not playing the same game you want at recess. Often we let students brainstorm situations that have occurred or that they think may occur and use those as lessons.

- **Flexibility in the real world**: Make the connection to how adults have to be flexible in real life situations. When using careers or job responsibilities the connection is made to life outside the classroom and in the real world. You can even use a topic that is a current event to use as a topic. One year we used the tsunami hitting Japan as a topic and brainstormed ways people in those cities as well as surrounding cities and countries had to be or could be flexible. These kinds of simulations really open the minds of the students to thinking outside of their immediate, often limited, world.

- **Flexible scheduling**: Does your schedule ever get changed? Do you and the students have to be flexible to accommodate this change? Make it a lesson or a discussion. Turn it into something positive. Are there ways that you can alter your schedule to meet the needs of the students? Any half-day we have on our school calendar means that we have an altered schedule. This also means that we have to be flexible and modify where we are with our teaching. I am very fortunate to work with an amazing group of teachers who are flexible and we make these days a blast for the students. We change up their class dynamics and move students around. We teach collaborative and themed lessons that enhance anything that we are doing within our regular curriculum. Being flexible has allowed for the learning to reach higher levels and helped to instill excitement and passion within our classrooms.

- **Changing assignments**: Start off with an assignment, like writing a short story or developing a skit. However, in the middle of the assignment, have students or groups switch their work with another group to finish. While some may grumble or complain, most will find it a fun twist and adapt to the new assignment.

Key Points to Remember

- Be willing to modify and adjust when needed.
- Model examples of when you have to be flexible and that will help them to also learn the skill.
- Try not to get upset and think you have failed. Stay positive and solve the problem.
- Set guidelines for communicating with students, parents, and other teachers. This will help to let them know when you will respond to them. They will feel validated and you will not be expected to be available at every whim.
- Be willing to examine your own decisions and accept when something has gone wrong. Denial is not a productive aspect to have in a classroom.
- Think of students first. There are times when their needs supersede ours and we need to put them first. (I have often adjusted due dates if students need more time with a project. I was willing to be flexible for the benefit of the student.)
- Reinforce that flexibility is needed in the real world by making connections to problem solving opportunities that occur within the classroom, such as accepting other view points, negotiating with others, and responding to needs or interest of others.
- Flexibility is what enables individuals to generate new ways to solve a problem, adapt to changes in routines, and adjust to the unexpected.
- Flexibility is a valued characteristic of leaders, so help your students develop this leadership trait.

14 Create Kids of Character

> "To educate a man in mind and not in morals is to educate a menace to society."
>
> Theodore Roosevelt

Our Thoughts and Some Research Too

One of the goals of public education is to prepare "productive citizens." While this sounds like an admirable pursuit for any mission statement, exactly what is a productive citizen? This is someone who gives back to society and takes an active role in improving the community. The best way to improve a community is to live a life of good character. It is the most important gift you can give yourself and it will benefit you in every aspect of your life. Besides the individual, character is also essential for our society to function effectively. When you don't exhibit good character, other people get hurt and yourself as well. Your integrity is your most important virtue.

The quote above by Roosevelt shows what happens when we no longer focus on the values of character, integrity, and morals. Sixty years ago, character was taught routinely in churches, homes, and even schools. Children growing up in those times had a reference point. Today, "moral character" (teaching students to do the honest, ethical, and right things) is rarely taught in our schools. Instead, our schools are teaching "performance character" (teaching students to maximize their performance – achieving "good grades" and "high test scores"). In reality, students, as well as adults, need both.

Today, individuals in our society are taught that achieving "success" is more important than how that success is achieved. That obtaining an outcome is more important than how you got there and the principles to which you adhere. In a recent survey by the Josephson Institute of Ethics, 70 percent of the high school students surveyed admitted that they cheat in school, but 91 percent said that they were satisfied with their own ethics and character. Yet 97 percent said that it is important for a person to be a person of good character! Children are being conditioned to cheat in order to succeed in athletics and the business world. Businessmen defraud their shareholders for personal gain. Even politicians, who are supposed to be servants of the people, cannot be trusted to do what they said they would do.

Even within the educational field, instances of cheating have become all too common. There have been entire school districts under investigation for widespread cheating on standardized tests. Sadly, in some cases, it wasn't just one or two people, but many people who were actively involved in the cheating scandal, or knew about it and did nothing. How can these administrators, teachers, and education in general expect to produce students with integrity and good character when they don't demonstrate it themselves.

While success is highly valued, character should be more highly valued. We often view success as reaching a certain level in business, sports, the world of celebrities, or some other field. However, this type of success is what I consider secondary greatness. Secondary greatness is more about "doing" as someone's source of identity, such as becoming a CEO, getting drafted by a sports team, or even becoming a famous singer. However, what we do is different from what we are, or our "being." This is referred to, by Steven Covey, as our "primary greatness." Primary greatness is what is on the inside: your character, values, morals, and integrity. Unfortunately, most people are raised in a comparison-based culture, so the focus is more on secondary greatness, to become rich and famous, rather than primary greatness, which deals with character and contribution to society.

The difference between primary and secondary greatness is similar to the difference between self-worth and self-esteem. Self-worth is your sense of self, your overall feeling of importance and value in this world, while self-esteem is a favorable opinion of yourself based on your actions. Usually when there is a conversation about children it is focused upon self-esteem, such as every child should get a trophy for participating because it will boost his/her self-esteem.

However, in most cases we tend to nurture the self-esteem in a manner which is not compatible with the very nature of self-esteem. Remember, self-esteem is about doing, not being. So, one has to accomplish goals to boost self-esteem, not simply show up. This is why it's important to have high expectations of students in the classroom and emphasize the importance of hard work. Hard work is in itself a reward and a boost to our self-esteem. However, self-worth is rarely addressed, especially with students. What do we value in the classroom? Good grades? Students who sit at their desks and never talk? What about all the other students? What about students who are positive, helpful, or encouraging? Is their self-worth being reinforced?

Researchers Joan E. Grusec and Erica Redler investigated what happens when we commend generous behavior versus generous character. The researchers randomly assigned the children to receive different types of praise. For some of the children, they praised the action: "It was good that you gave some of your marbles to those poor children. Yes, that was a nice and helpful thing to do." For others, they praised the character behind the action: "I guess you're the kind of person who likes to help others whenever you can. Yes, you are a very nice and helpful person."

A couple of weeks later, when faced with more opportunities to give and share, the children were much more generous after their character had been praised than after their actions had been. Praising their character helped them internalize it as part of their identities. The children learned who they were from observing their own actions: I am a helpful person. This dovetails with new research led by the psychologist Christopher J. Bryan, who finds that for moral behaviors, nouns work better than verbs. To get 3- to 6-year-olds to help with a task rather than inviting them "to help," it was 22 to 29 percent more effective to encourage them to "be a helper." Cheating was cut in half when instead of, "Please don't cheat," participants were told, "Please don't be a cheater."

Do you see the difference and the dilemma? Asking a child to not be a cheater would be seen by some as harming the child's self-esteem while the research suggests that it will actually improve the behavior. When our actions become a reflection of our character, we lean more heavily toward the moral and generous choices. Over time it can become part of us. Isn't this the type of citizens that we want in our communities and societies?

By now you recognize that the productive citizen, mentioned in the beginning of the section, is best described as a person of character. The Josephson Institute of Ethics identifies the "Pillars of Character" as trustworthiness, respect, responsibility, fairness, caring, and citizenship. So, how can we be educating "productive citizens" if we are not developing their character?

Dr. Deborah Gilboa, national parenting expert, believes that developing children of character is as important as learning the basics or reading, writing, and arithmetic. She said when we focus only on concepts like self-esteem we are singularly focused on making "happy" kids. As she said, "It is easy to make students happy, simply give them some candy and let them watch cartoons on television." However, we owe our children more than to simply be happy, we need to help them develop character so students feel good by doing rather than just receiving. She shared the story of a young man she had met while speaking at a school. She asked what he enjoyed doing for fun and he said he loved riding his horse. But, he said he only got to ride the horse after he had finished his chores every day. She said he quickly named off about seven chores that he did daily such as clearing breakfast dishes, cleaning the horse stalls, and feeding the horses. He didn't complain but realized that was part of the process. He was developing character because his happiness was derived from what he was doing, not simply receiving something.

While parents from an early age should develop character, it can be reinforced in the school as well. In fact, in some instances, the teacher may be the only positive role model in a child's life. Dr. Elizabeth Berger, noted child psychiatrist, explains, "In the classroom it is not a lesson, but the teacher who plays a role in developing the character of her students." Dr. Berger continues, "character skills are abstract, not concrete, so trying to 'teach' the concept of character to children is a daunting task . . .. It is more effective to emulate character traits and create an atmosphere in the classroom and school where character is emphasized. For instance, a teacher can establish an atmosphere where students don't interrupt other students and people aren't criticized for having a different point of view."

While it is essential to respect each other, it is also important to respect processes, such as group work, citizenship, and relationships. When a positive environment is created, there is a sense of pride in the class and the classroom becomes a meaningful place to be. This positive environment empowers students and gives them a sense of hope, rather than a sense of helplessness. This environment creates the opportunity for students to act right, do right, and develop their character. This is not something that can be taught in a lesson or on a test, but it is lived out daily by choices you as a teacher or parent make, and that the students make. Living with good character should not be a rarity, but rather it should be commonplace, regardless of the student's age.

However, when someone does portray high character it seems more like an anomaly rather than the norm. I remember in 2010 when San Francisco Giants pitcher Jeremy Affeldt was overpaid by $500,000.00 because of a clerical error in his contract. When he received his paystub, he realized that he had been overpaid. He questioned the club and his agent about the error. The error was part of the contract, so legally he could keep the money. Affeldt recalled Michael Moye (his agent) telling him, "You know what? As your agent I've got to tell you that legally you can keep it. As a man who represents integrity, I'm saying you should give it back." Affeldt said he told the Giants organization, "I can't take that money," he said. "I won't sleep well at night knowing I took that money because every time I open my paycheck I'll know it's not right." This was a situation where Affeldt not only had a chance to keep half a million dollars, more than some people make in a lifetime, but he actually had the law on his side. However, he lives his life focused more on "primary" greatness than "secondary" greatness and he knew it would be wrong to keep the money. What a great example of character and doing the right thing.

Did you know?

Only 12 states in the Unites States require character to be taught within the curriculum of the schools. http://www.cbsnews.com/news/teaching-character-in-school

Personal Experiences and Stories

Our school has a motto that we encourage all students to follow. It is W.A.T.C.H. It stands for Words, Actions, Thoughts, Character, and Habits. To us that represents the types of students we want within our school and it shows what type of people we want our students to become when they leave and go on in life. Our school has also adopted a program on virtues for our younger students with it continuing in different ways throughout grades 1–12. Grades and academic performance are a top priority for our teachers, students, and parents. We are a college preparatory school. But, character also matters. It is what makes our students productive citizens. The academic content prepares them for their profession, but the character piece gives them tools to succeed within that profession and society.

With my own students, I (Julie) have a W.A.T.C.H. box where students can fill out forms and put in. The forms are evidence of when students caught each other exhibiting positive W.A.T.C.H. characteristics. Students write the name of the student, the action observed, and the letter to which it connects. Then they sign their name. At class meetings we share forms from the W.A.T.C.H. box. Not only does this recognize the positive character trait that the student exhibited, it models it for others, and also recognizes the student that acknowledged the trait. When students can acknowledge others performing the traits then it means they truly understand the characteristics of that trait. This also models to all students that while we care about their academic success, we also value their character.

Another great way for students to focus on good citizenship/character building is to do fundraisers or find a local charity to help out. Several years ago I (Brad) taught at a school that was near a food pantry. It was during a time when the economy had worsened and there were a lot of families in the area who were relying on the food pantry just to feed their children. I decided to have the operations manager come speak to our high school students. She gave a presentation and explained the dire straits that some families were in and how important the food pantry was in helping these people survive and keep their dignity.

The students were emotionally affected by the presentation and wanted to know how they could help. So, I decided to take one of my classes to the food pantry to work for a couple of afternoons. They loved the experience. Several of my students spoke Spanish, so they were able to help any families who couldn't speak English, but spoke only Spanish. They cleaned, bagged up groceries for families, and helped restock the shelves. However, while we were there, we noticed the shelves were really bare. So, the students asked me if they could do a fundraiser to help the food pantry.

I gave them the opportunity to come up with a way to raise food for the pantry. I knew this was something they were now passionate about and I wanted them to step up as leaders and make decisions. They decided to ask students to bring in canned goods in exchange for a hat day, where they could wear a hat in the classrooms. The students could purchase the food themselves or go into the community and ask for donations. We set a time later the next week and students brought in enough canned and boxed food to fill a small bus. The food pantry estimated we delivered between 4,000–6,000 lbs of food to the pantry and they actually gave a certificate to the group of students who worked and helped with the food drive. Many of the students continued to volunteer at the food pantry on their own time and every year they continued to do a food drive for the pantry. At the end of the day, it is not what students make on a standardized test which will influence how successful they are in life, but it will be the empathy, integrity, and character that they exhibit. The goal of education should be to develop students who exhibit primary greatness.

Did you know?

Teaching character in our schools is not a new concept. Horace Mann advocated for character to be taught nationwide back in the 1840s. http://www.cbsnews.com/news/teaching-character-in-school

Ideas to Try

- **Brainstorm and define character traits**: Let students create a list of terms and have them try to define each with examples. Then use these for discussions or lessons. For example, talk to your students about what integrity means, and what it means to stand up for your own values. Ask them who they see as having a sense of integrity, and who they think backs down from their values in the face of adversity. Responsibility is another character trait. Help students understand the keys to responsibility. Here are a few of the examples my students came up with to describe the keys to responsibility: Be reliable and dependable; when you agree to do something, do it. Take care of your own business. Don't make others do what you are supposed to do. Take responsibility for your actions; don't make excuses or blame others. Use your head; think before you act; imagine the consequences.

- **Examine role models**: Have students brainstorm a list of role models and then examine each one using the traits that the school has adopted or the ones you have brainstormed. Students naturally choose role models in their lives. Help them to recognize the traits that made them choose those particular people in their lives. Make an effort to point out positive character role models in history, literature, science, and the arts. Deliberately teach about people that your students can emulate. Ask students to describe, assess, and match the traits and behaviors of these people or commendable characters within a fiction story. They could even dramatize some of the story elements or change them to allow a character to make better choices.

- **Create a culture of respect**: Your classroom should be firmly established on a foundation of respect. Self-respect and respect for others are the basis of all other positive character traits. Negativity and abuse of any kind should not be tolerated, and met with appropriate consequences. Create an environment where the virtues of treating all classmates with respect and dignity are desirable.

- **Choose a character theme to focus on throughout the month or year**: The theme for my classroom is respect. At every possible chance I get I recognize aspects of respect. We must respect each other in order to successfully complete science labs, our selves in every aspect of what we do, and nature. The connection to nature really makes an impact on my students. They are between 10 and 11 years old and by now they know they should respect themselves and one another. But bringing in nature takes it to a whole new level. It makes a connection that really makes a difference in how they look at the world.

- **Volunteer**: Take time in your classroom to highlight the virtues and importance of volunteerism. Start volunteer programs in your classroom and school. Help at a local food bank, assist with reading comprehension or provide support for students recovering from an illness or injury. I set up food can drives for our local food bank and allowed students to work at the food bank occasionally to "give back" to the community.

- Have the kids **role play** or use puppets to act out the following situation: Four good friends are planning to spend a day at an amusement park. Two of them want to invite another kid who's new in school. The other two don't want to include this person because he/she is different in some way (different race, a "dweeb," from a foreign country, etc.). After the role play have a class discussion. Then, have four others do another role play changing what it is that's different about the new kid. Repeat this process changing the difference each time.

- **Story tell or read stories** about situations of character or lack of character. These can be fictitious or real life stories. Read aloud or have students read stories on their own. Our school has summer reading requirements. We have a character book that we hope each family will read together. Last year it was *Wonder* by R. J. Palacio. Read it. It will change your life. It made a huge impact on our school community.

- **Bring in articles from newspapers** and magazines describing situations in which respect or disrespect are issues. Talk about who is acting respectfully, and who is acting disrespectfully in these situations. Politics is one area where disrespect seems to be all too common. There are many examples in the news of politicians acting out in inappropriate ways.

- **Problem finder**: We are trained to be problem solvers, but a different take on this is for students to be problem finders. Allow students to find an issue in the classroom, such as it takes too long to line up for music, or that they are late to lunch often. The teacher is usually quick to come up with solutions, but why not let students identify such problems and then come up with solutions. Try each of their solutions for a period of time and then incorporate the best one.

- **Otherness**: Human nature is to be self-centered, or at least ego-centric, we tend to view the world in regards to ourselves. One activity to help students focus on others is to have them find out the names and birthdays of all the school staff (such as custodians, lunchroom workers, etc.). Then the students can make a birthday card for each staff member on their birthdate. This is a great way to show that every person is important regardless of position and that everyone should be treated the same.

- **Empathy** is the ability to understand another person's experience and emotions. This is important for students to learn. Incorporate active listening to help develop empathy. Such as don't interrupt when someone is speaking, listen carefully, and maintain eye contact. Teach students to encourage and praise each other, this is not the sole responsibility of the teacher. Students also need to learn to give full attention to someone, not distracted by emails, texts, or something else.

Key Points to Remember

- Be a good example. Model good character for your students. Are you walking the walk?

- Make character education the foundation of your class, not just a lesson that you teach.

- Show respect to students and others, such as staff. Respect is really the beginning of education.

- Use language which helps them understand good character. Children cannot develop a moral compass unless people around them use clear, sharp language of right and wrong.

- Give the students responsibilities in the classroom. Ownership and work ethic are important to developing good character.

- Be firm and consistent when students break rules or policies. Students need consequences to help define boundaries.

- Help students find their passion or provide opportunities for them to express their passion in the classroom.

- Find ways to team up with parents to reinforce good behavior and doing things the right way.

15 | Integrate Technology

"Never doubt that a small group of thoughtful, committed citizens can change the world. Indeed, it is the only thing that ever has."

Margaret Mead

Our Thoughts and Some Research Too

Technology is a part of our everyday life, whether we want to admit it or not. How we go through our typical day today is very different than how we went through the day when we were in school and an almost unrecognizable world than when our parents were in school. Keep that mindset for a moment and compare it to our children. What is to say that the world won't be just as different for them when they become adults? Can you even imagine the technology that will be designed? So keeping with that mindset, aren't we doing our students a disservice if we don't integrate technology in every meaningful way? How can we adequately prepare them to succeed in an ever-changing world if we don't teach them to use the tools we have available now?

Doug Bergman, Microsoft in Education Global Forum award winner, shared that regardless of what country we come from, what culture we grow up in, or what economic conditions we live in, we all must solve the problems in our homes, cities, states, countries, and our global world. We need tools in order to do that. And the tools of today are digital. He went on to state that, "the people who are in command of those digital tools will be the leaders of innovation, academia, business, industry, politics, entertainment, research, and philanthropy."

Unfortunately, there are schools and even districts in countries around the globe which lack the technology to adequately prepare students with certain computer skills. This means we need to do a better job of getting technology in every school where children have the opportunity to build on these skills and compete in a technological world. This creates a wonderful opportunity where districts and schools can find corporations with which to partner to help improve the technology in the classrooms.

Doug, who is currently the Head of the Computer Science program at Porter-Gaud, has taken his philosophy of collaboration and integration of computer science and redesigned the approach used in his school. While the AP Curriculum still is a focus within some school systems today, he decided for a paradigm shift and threw out the AP mentality for a partnership with a local college and designed his own curriculum. His three-year program focuses on software development and problem solving through game design, robotics, apps, simulations, and websites.

Computer science skills should not be for the technologically elite, but they should be, and can be, skills for everyone. Just as we use writing and reading to learn and express our ideas, we need Computer Science to be an additional tool that students can use to get their ideas across, introduce possible solutions, analyze problems, make new tools, and actually produce something that people in the real world can use to address the issues around them.

When Doug refers to solving issues, he means on the local, regional, national and international stages. His students are not confined to walls within a classroom and don't experience borders or boundaries. His students interact with industry experts and even collaborate on projects with real organizations, such as the Charleston Association for the Blind. Here are some of the topics in which his students created games or interactive simulations: poverty, natural disaster, nuclear testing, tsunami alert, suicide, animal cruelty, anorexia, access to food and water in third world countries, sports injuries, medical training, Olympics security, terrorism, farm soil deterioration, healthy food habits, bicycle accidents on roadways, and deforestation. It's crucial that students research and pick their topic so that they "buy into" the context of their game. The Computer Science will come naturally because that is exactly how they will make their game do what they want it to do. And the same Computer Science skills that are involved in games are used in software development in any industry.

These students are developing their passions, opinions of the world, their place in the world, and the things that they care about – don't we want them thinking about worldly issues and expressing their views about them?

We don't normally give the younger generation the chance to express their ideas about real-worldly issues, when in fact we find that they care deeply about making the world a better place. They have a great deal to say about it. Based on the caliber and quality of the projects submitted, they are very eager and excited to express and share their ideas. Maybe the game or activity that they create will be a step towards a career that tackles their chosen problem. It is this connection to the real world that needs to be implemented within our schools.

So is it just playing with a computer all day? Many skeptics will ask: what about the basics? Don't our students need to learn to read, write, and do math? Aren't we trying to keep up and compete with countries all over the world for rankings and for jobs? Yes, we are. We are not just trying to keep up, but we are trying to regain our leadership in this global economy. The countries that embrace innovation, maximize their technology, and solve problems will be the ones that lead the world. We are preparing students for a worldwide market place and to function within a global economy. All of these topics require hours and hours of research. Reading, writing, math, and more are all components of the game design. Even better than the basics are the idea that the students are learning to think on their own, problem solve, and present their work and efforts.

These students are spending weeks researching about and connecting with something that is important to them and they are engaged the entire time. Some students seem to dedicate every waking moment to getting their project to work like THEY want it. They will come in early, stay late, come in at study hall and lunch. Not because of a grade, most of the students accomplish the required components during class; what they do outside of class is just "extra" because they want to excel. Wow! Students going the extra mile not because of a grade, simply because they are engaged in their own learning and excited about expressing themselves in the exact way they want – and they have a tool at their fingertips to do just that.

Fortunately, many children are interacting with technology even more than adults. They have no fear of it. They are growing up with it. To them it is a normal part of their daily life. So then, why isn't it an integral part of the school day? Children are passionate about technology and excited when using it. Don't we want that passion and excitement transferred into our classrooms and schools? There is age-appropriate game development and technology use that can easily be implemented within the classrooms.

In schools today we often live by schedules and routines. Unfortunately it is still very much like an assembly line. When are the students really given opportunities to think on their own and have a say in their own learning process? This is where computer science comes in. For most students as long as they can remember, they are told what to do every day of their life. From the moment they wake up, they are told what to wear, where to go, when to go, when to stop, what and when to eat, what to do when they get there.

Now think of a Computer Science project. There is not necessarily any one answer to our problems and projects. In fact, even what we are assigning can be interpreted differently. Finally, the students are in control of their own learning. They get to decide exactly what the computer will do, how it will do it, how long it will do it, and how it will communicate that it did it. And they can change it right there and instantly see the effect. They can fine-tune it, or they can overhaul the entire project. It is because students take ownership of their own learning. They are doing it because they are curious, not just to see if they can, but how well they can, and then what else can they do to make it even better. This is differentiated instruction at its best!

As educators it is our job to prepare our students for the future. While we cannot possibly know the problems industries will face in the future or the kind of technology that will be designed, it is safe to say digital devices of some sort will be involved. We need to create learning environments where students have been given the tools needed to think, create, modify, adjust, and generate ideas. It is safe to say that the students leaving this type of computer science class can take ideas in their heads and bring them to life on a screen or device in their hands. They are ready for the real world. Are your students?

Did you know?

The Bureau of Labor Statistics projects that by the year 2020 there will be 4.2 million jobs in computing and information technology in the U.S., putting these fields among the fastest growing occupational fields. www.computinginthecore.org/facts-resource

Personal Experiences and Stories

I (Julie) have the fortunate opportunity to work at Porter Gaud along with Doug Bergman. He has inspired me to incorporate computer science in the classroom, and now, I can't imagine teaching without it. To me computer science goes beyond using iPads, tablets, laptops or computers. Those tools should already be integrated fluidly within schools. That is a given. Those types of technology are already regularly used by most outside of the classroom, so it only makes sense to also use them as tools within the classroom. That is where I started and then I grew from there. Daily my students use their apps on their iPads, send and receive emails, and pretty much don't go a day without interacting with some type of technology. So I took it from there and dove into the realm of computer science.

The first program I used, and continue to use, is SCRATCH. This is a drag and drop gaming program designed by MIT that allows students to code their own games or simulations. I was shocked when I first offered a class to 9 and 10 year olds and the registration list became so long that another class had to be created. I was a novice, to say the least, at coding and easily learned along with my students. The games they produced were incredible. I had a group of advanced students who wanted to add Xbox Kinect to the programing. So what did we do? We Skyped with the person who wrote the code for that type of gaming and figured out how to do it. Mind you, he lives in England so we did have to factor in the time difference, but what a real-life experience for these 10-year-olds.

After experiencing the passion and joy for learning from teaching that class, I decided coding needed to be a permanent part of my science curriculum. That is when I incorporated SCRATCH into every class I taught. We used SCRATCH to simulate interaction within ecosystems. Every 10–11 year old student in the past three years in my class has had the opportunity to design and publish a game while learning about ecosystems and habitats. They loved it! But as times change, so must we. There is an app called Hopscotch. That is our newest addition to science class. The students use the same principles that they learned with coding SCRATCH and code pictures, games, and simulations on the app. Again, they love it. We had actual lessons that I created to go along with the science content, but four months later I still see the students on the app any free time they have. It is like they crave the opportunity to design and generate something new.

So we continue to code . . . and code . . . and code! What child doesn't like Legos? In our Lower School we have a Lego robotics program for ages 6–12. Students have the opportunity to experience project-based, interdisciplinary lessons through the use of Legos. Depending on the age, the students problem solve for real-world issues, design and build structures with moving parts, compete, and present. The engineering aspect of our science curriculum has been enhanced through computer science.

> ### *Did you know?*
>
> Several major universities around the world have temporarily banned iPad use because of bandwidth overload. The universities cannot keep up with the usage! http://www.zdnet.com/blog/igeneration/open-letter-university-ipad-ban-catch-up-simple-as/4683

Ideas to Try

- **Be comfortable with basic technology**: This is the place to start. Most people have not grown up with the type of technology that is used today. You need to dive right in and immerse yourself in the world of the students in regards to technology. Use iPads, explore websites and social media sites, play video games. It is important you see the world through the eyes of your students to understand where they are coming from. But, also embrace that your students might know more about something than you. How they love to show the teacher something! In fact, challenge your students to teach you new things as often as possible. At every level within our school we have students who share what they have learned or figured out, often including better ways to do things. I love those moments!

- **Integrate basic technology within your class first**: If you have never cooked before then you are not going to apply to be a chef at a restaurant. The same goes with technology. You must first become comfortable with the devices and concepts before you start some major new adventure into the world of technology. This doesn't mean that you can't learn along with the students. That is to be expected. But get familiar with iPads before you use apps in your classroom. Research the apps before you purchase too many or unneeded ones. That will save your school lots of money. The storage space alone for unwanted apps that have been downloaded needs to be taken into consideration. Just like prepping for any lesson you teach, you need to be comfortable using the tools that are needed for the lesson to be successful. It is hard to make a list of the "best" apps because new apps are being created all of the time. Remember this is an evolving and ever-changing field. We are continually researching and adding programs to our fluid list which we use in our classrooms. The App Store has categories for education that will help you figure out what is best for you. To give you a head start, here is a list of the basic programs that we have found to enhance learning. You will need to research and find specific subject area programs/apps that will enhance your classroom.

- Coding: SCRATCH (website), Hopscotch (app), Tynker (app)
- Creativity: iMovie, Educreations (app), ShowMe (app), Book Creator (app), StoryBuilder (app), QRCreator (app), SmartMusic (app)
- Planner/Organization: iStudiezPro (app), planbook.com (website), Notability (app), Dropbox (app), Evernote (app), Flashcardlet (app)
- Educational: Pages (app), Keynote (app), Numbers (app), KidsDiscover (app), Explain Everything (app), Edmodo (app and website), iTunesU (app)

- **Design and implement a school-wide technology plan**: Does your school allow the use of cell phones? Are you a 1–1 iPad program? Can students carry their own laptops? Does your school use Moodle? Facebook? Twitter? Instagram? What is appropriate for you to use with the students? These are just a few of numerous questions that schools today are addressing. The groundwork and boundaries need to be laid first and then the technology can be used in a safe manner. We need to remember that these are children and we are exposing them to devices that often do not have the safe boundaries in which we would like them to navigate. Be careful about arbitrary rules and regulations. Don't look for ways to limit technology, look for ways to increase productive use.

- **Implement at every grade level**: Find ways to first implement technology and then to integrate computer science within the curriculum at every grade level. This can start with things as basic as iMovie and QR codes. It doesn't matter how basic, just start and then grow from there. When students first start school they should be exposed to educational software that reinforces reading and math skills. They should be using digital cameras, interactive whiteboards, multimedia encyclopedias and dictionaries, and also be introduced to the Internet. (I find that amazing because that sounds like what I started doing when I was in college! But, times are changing and so must our mindset of technology in the classroom.)

- **Allow students an opportunity to work with devices with which they are familiar and can enhance development**: Our younger students work with Legos and on SCRATCH and Hopscotch. In science class we also use the Xbox Kinect. Our students have also partnered with the high school students (ages 15–16) for consultation on their Xbox Kinect programing game design class. Students at our school also design apps for Android, take apart and rebuild desktop and laptop computers, and design websites on real-web servers.

- **Introduce students to real-world technology and software**: It is crucial students have a chance to explore not only software development in different environments, but also have a chance to work with a variety of devices on which that software runs. Students should get to explore creating programs that use a variety of inputs such as body gestures, brain waves, or audio – so that the people that are working with them can include people of limited physical capabilities such as the visually impaired, amputees, or those with limited movement. Students should also have experience working with other output devices besides screens, such as robots (which are used in almost every industry), tablets and smartphones, and sensor equipment.

- **Communicate through technology**: This should be a focus when integrating computer science into your classroom. Whether they write a story, draw a picture, present to a panel of judges, train someone to create their own app, make a product, or develop a game . . . they are communicating an idea that they have that is their own – something that they thought about, developed in their head, and then produced a tangible "something" that expresses that idea to others. With digital devices being as common as they are, those who can produce digital solutions are the ones who will reach more people faster and across borders.

Key Points to Remember

- Technology is a part of our everyday life and needs to be a part of our school systems, too.
- Technology integration should include having a meaningful, school-wide plan to ensure safety of the students using the technology.
- Start with becoming comfortable with using basic technology in the classroom and becoming familiar with technology that your students are using.
- Integrate that technology within the core subject areas.
- Add coding, programing, and design within the curriculum.

16 | **Promote Teamwork**

" The strength of the team is each individual member. The strength of each member is the team."

Phil Jackson

Our Thoughts and Some Research Too

Imagine walking into your workplace with huge open spaces, bright colors, booths, tables, and conference areas only separated by glass. Technology can be incorporated wherever and whenever needed. Would you like a fully functioning gourmet kitchen, food stations stocked for your enjoyment, a work out facility, a convenience store, a credit union, and even a nurse on staff? This is what I saw when I walked in the Kraft Foods Group building in Northfield, Chicago. As I walked up, I saw products that represented the company (I have to admit I took a picture with the Kool-Aid man coming out of the wall), beautifully maintained grounds, and smiling employees. Kraft Foods Group represents the type of company that promotes a healthy, collaborative work environment where the employees come first.

Kraft Foods Group is a Fortune 500 North American company with revenues upwards of 18 billion dollars last year alone. Kraft products are in approximately 98 percent of North American households and it is the fifth most recognized group worldwide. Within the past several years, Kraft has generated a philosophy that promotes teamwork and sustainability. To make this shift, Kraft has redesigned buildings and altered the culture within the workplace. Kraft had traditional office spaces for years with the plush, expansive, executive offices on their own floor and floor after floor of closed off cubicles, office, and cubbies. Kraft was structured like most traditional companies across the world. That type of environment did not promote engagement and interaction.

Diane Johnson May, the Vice President of Human Resources, said that people would walk by her office and never come in to talk. They would send her an email instead of face-to-face conversations. She recognized that this culture needed to change and was in support of the multi-million dollar renovation of the facilities. Kraft made a conscious effort to create a paradigm shift of removing the hierarchical structure and creating an "open space" concept. There were several goals associated with the Open Space concept, which included sustainability, collaboration, and creating a culture of teamwork. She says that now people walk up to her and engage in conversation and share ideas. The entire culture of the company has changed to promote collaboration.

She shared that people within the company all have individual responsibilities with performance evaluations, but these employees all bring their strengths to the group and experience success as a team. Diane also shared that when interviewing they look to hire people who are willing to work on a team and who can provide evidence of successful teamworking opportunities in which they have experience. This only strengthens the fact that we need to give students the opportunity to work in collaborative groups and promote teamwork within our schools. It is already being adopted within major corporations. We are doing our students a disservice if we are not adequately preparing them for the real world.

Teamwork has become such an integral part of the business world that Fortune 500 companies will frequently visit collegiate sports teams to see the infrastructure of how a successful team works. For example, Dell and HCA and other companies will visit teams like The Vanderbilt Commodores because they know that students who participate in sports tend to have great teamwork skills which are highly valued in the workplace.

One of the greatest teams in the world is the SEAL Team, which springs from the military. Function independently and failure is imminent. Function as a team and success is possible. Teamwork is a fundamental concept within the military, whether it is in the US, UK or anywhere in the world. Each member has a specific role to play that adds to the entire group. The group's goal is larger than the individual goal, but it is the combined talents of the individuals that make the goals attainable.

Many teachers do group activities, but developing activities where students work as a team is different than just placing students in a group. I'm reminded of the comedian that talked about the reading groups when he was in school. He said the high reading group was called the "Soaring Eagles" and the low reading group was called . . . Group 2. The comedian happened to be in the low group and joked about the lack of emphasis placed on naming his group or the work done in the group. A group has characteristics such as: members are given their tasks or told what their job is in the group, members work independently and they often are not working towards the same goal, members may have a lot to contribute but are held back because they were given a specific task, and members may or may not participate in group decision making if it even exists.

A team has characteristics that are different from a group. This doesn't mean that groups are bad or that there isn't a place for group work, because groups are often utilized in the school setting. However, teams have traits that have more specific goals to achieve. The following are characteristics of teamwork or team building:

- Provides an opportunity for students to offer their skills and knowledge, and they in turn are able contribute to the group's success.
- Students work interdependently and work towards both personal and team goals. When students work as a team, they feel a sense of ownership because they commit themselves to goals they helped create.
- Students collaborate together and use their talent and experience to contribute to the success of the team's goals.
- Members participate equally in decision making, but each member understands that the leader might need to make the final decision if there is no group consensus.

Therefore, it is important that students learn to function in a team environment so that they will be more successful when they enter the workforce. Research also suggests that students learn best from doing activities that involve social interactions. Some of the benefits of teamwork include:

- increases motivation
- improves productivity
- fosters problem-solving skills
- encourages creativity
- allows students to exhibit their individual talents and abilities
- allows the students to feel part of a bigger thing than just an individual

An important characteristic of teamwork or team-building exercises is that some students will be leaders in certain activities and may be followers in another. This allows students who are quiet and shy the opportunity to step up when an activity suits their talents and skills while continually building self-confidence. Teamwork activities also allow students who may not excel academically to step up as leaders by utilizing other talents or skills that will be helpful to the team.

The types of activities will depend on the age of the students. Not every team-building activity requires all the characteristics of teamwork describer earlier. Remember, the key is to develop skills that will help students succeed in life. Some activities can be directly related to the class, like using the calculator, or others may be activities that focus solely on team building. Even though the activity may not be subject area specific, the skill of learning teamwork is valid for any subject area at any age.

Did you know?

Japanese writer Ryunosuke Satoro once said, "Individually, we are one drop. Together, we are an ocean." http://money.howstuffworks.com/business/starting-a-job/how-to-improve-teamwork-in-workplace.htm

Personal Experiences and Stories

I (Julie) have taught for over 20 years and have had students participate in both group work and teamwork. There is a noticeable difference with the students' attitudes and the end result when they are put in a team. It is like they become part of a bigger thing than just being an individual. They belong to a group, even if just for a little while, that has a specific goal or challenge. More times than not I have witnessed success beyond what I ever expected. Lower students build confidence and the higher-level students share knowledge. Everyone brings something different to the team and everyone has his or her own strengths, which ultimately makes the team better as a whole.

Last year we did an Olympics unit for an entire grade level of students. In total there were 72 students split into teams representing different countries. One country had not yet won a medal and we were on Day 3. That country did not give up, but instead revised plans and encouraged each other in every activity in which they participated. They seemed to grow stronger and more focused. When the first event took place on Day 4 they won the gold. They hugged each other and celebrated like they had won real gold medals. All of the teammates wore the medals all day and then hung them in their lockers. Their sense of pride and accomplishment even astonished the teachers. Each one of those students walked taller that day and it was because they experienced success as a team.

Did you know?

Teamwork doesn't mean that individuals have to set aside their personal goals for the good of the group. The best team enhances each person's abilities. http://money.howstuffworks.com/business/starting-a-job/how-to-improve-teamwork-in-workplace.htm

Ideas to Try

Some examples of team-building activities would include:

- **Dictionary Debate**: This is a game that helps students develop vocabulary and word skills. Each student has a white board and marker, or notebook paper will do. They are divided into two teams. The teacher chooses a word such as "jump." She will then ask for a synonym or an antonym. Each team is given a point for each correct answer. However, if an answer is duplicated within a team then the answer is thrown out, and no point is given. For instance, if the teacher asks for a synonym for the word "jump" and more than one person on the same team answers "leap," then no point is awarded. This rule helps stretch the vocabulary of the students.

- **Building Blind**: For Building Blind, students work in groups of three or more. One student is the leader and the others are an engineer or builders. The leader can see a simple structure (usually made of Legos or other building blocks), but the engineer and builders can't see it. The leader must explain to the engineers how to recreate the structure and which pieces to use. The engineer must then explain to the builders but cannot touch the pieces, so good communication skills are important. This activity can be related to science because of the engineering connection, but can be used simply for team-building skills.

- **Egg Drop**: Small groups design an egg package to save an egg from breaking when dropped. Plus they must also create a 30 second jingle to sell their package. The students perform the jingle and then it is followed by the Great Egg Drop-Off, which includes dropping the egg from a specific site at the school. This activity would be suited for a science or math class by making connections to measurement and Newton's Laws.

- **Magic Shoes**: Set the boundary lines about 4 feet apart. Have the team stand behind one boundary, while facing the other. Tell the team all the directions. The entire team must get from one boundary to the other and in between boundaries is a pit. The only way to get across is by using the invisible magic shoes (any pair of shoes). The goal is for all players to end up on the other side.

  1. Everyone must wear the shoes one time going one way.

  2. Shoes may not be tossed back to the other side

  3. Once you have worn the shoes you may not wear them again

  4. The same person must wear both shoes.

  5. Everyone works as a team to figure out a plan and a solution.

- **Roller Coaster Build**: This science-specific activity focuses on the concept of forces and motion. Students use Styrofoam tubes and marbles to create roller coasters. The team is given a set of challenges that they must overcome in order to be able to move to the next challenge. For example the first challenge is one hill and one turn, followed by two hills and two turns. Then one hill, one loop and one turn. The challenges continue until a complete roller coaster is built that can continue to run through the track over and over. Concepts such as Newton's Laws, potential and kinetic energy are focused on throughout the activity. The teams are given a certain time limit to plan and execute their designs. Points are awarded based on how many challenges were completed.

- **Interdisciplinary units where teams are required**: A unit that we have used with our students who range in age from 10 to 11 is based on the Olympics. Students are randomly assigned a country in which they have made the Olympic Team. Here are just a few challenges the students have completed as a team:

  o   Design a team flag (art teacher helps with this) and carry the flag in both the opening and closing ceremonies.

- ○ Write and perform a national theme song or anthem. (Our music teacher helps with this.)

- ○ Design the Olympic uniform (drawing on paper or iPads).

- ○ Compete in various events. (Metric Olympics based on AIMS activities.)

- ○ Compete in teacher-generated team-building events. (Our PE teachers join with the subject area teachers and help run events in the gym or outside.)

- The team members receive medals (paper with string) that they wear when they place first, second or third in an event. The medal count is recorded throughout the games just like it is in the Olympics. The duration of the unit depends on the teaching schedules, but we have found a week to be ideal.

- **Take a field trip** to a place where Low/High Ropes Courses are available: We plan overnight and day trips at various grade levels at our school to work on team-building skills. Students start at age 9 and then continue until age 16 to attend trips with opportunities to enhance team building.

FEEDBACK is ESSENTIAL! An important aspect with teamwork is for teachers to get feedback from teammates. I give a feedback form after every team-working activity that is completed in my class. Students know that I will only view these forms, so honesty is essential. This allows for me to have an insight to all aspects of the team. After reading the forms I can conference with the students individually and/or I can lead class discussions on positive aspects and challenges that arose with being a part of a team. I also take all of the forms from the entire team and average the numbers that were given to each individual team member. I track these numbers in a chart to see if there is growth. On the next page is the form that I use.

Rating of Teammates' Performance

Name _____ Activity _____ Group #_____

Please write the names of all of your team members, INCLUDING YOURSELF. Then write the number that best represents how the teammates completed their assigned tasks within the team. (This does not rate their academic ability.) Be sure to use the line provided to give specific examples. The possible ratings are as follows:

1 = Excellent	Consistently went above and beyond in regards to preparation and participation (tutored teammates if needed, picked up duties when others did not complete their own tasks). Was NOT bossy or overbearing.
2 = Very good	Consistently did what he/she was supposed to do, very well prepared, communicated well within the group.
3 = Average	At times did what he/she was supposed to do, but there were times when he/she had to be reminded to do their given tasks. Not very well prepared.
4 = Below Average	No participation, bossy, not working as a teammate.

Name of team member	Rating	Reason for Rating (specific examples)
_____	_____	_____
_____	_____	_____
_____	_____	_____
_____	_____	_____

Key Points to Remember

- Group work and teamwork are two totally different concepts with different characteristics and goals.

- Provide opportunities for students to showcase their talents and work towards a group goal.

- Plan events that are challenging and enjoyable for the students where they have time to complete the goals that were set.

- Team building is a skill for the future! So incorporate team building within subject areas for content-specific activities and then within any aspect of the curriculum possible. Make time for it!

- Provide feedback and work on team-building skills to help students grow and improve as teammates.

17 | **Teach Effective Communication**

" The way we communicate with others and with ourselves ultimately determines the quality of our lives."

Tony Robbins

Our Thoughts and Some Research Too

From the time we are born, we are able to communicate. Whether it is crying, smiling, frowning, hugging or even learning to speak, we are able to communicate with others. Even infants quickly bond with parents and siblings by making eye contact, recognizing faces, voice sounds, tone, and pitch. It seems to be so innate that we often forget that communication is a skill that can be developed just like any other skill.

As the quote above so accurately reflects, communication is probably the most important life skill we possess, and our quality of life is directly influenced by how well we can communicate. While we discuss developing talents throughout the book, all the talent in the world means little if you are not able to effectively communicate with others. When it comes to effective communication, there are two main types: verbal and nonverbal. Verbal communication includes talking, and written communication such as notes, emails, texts, etc. while nonverbal communication is our actions and expressions, which includes body language, tone of voice, eye contact, and facial expressions. Communication can be formal or informal in nature.

Formal communication is well thought out ways of transferring information. This often equates with meetings in the professional world and also within the school setting. This type of information is sent with the understanding that the content should be accurate with possible consequences if inaccurate. Informal communication occurs in settings that are associated with casual and relaxing environments. The information is not necessarily accurate or well thought out. No accountability is associated with informal communication. Finally, one of the most important and overlooked aspects of communication is listening. If we don't purposely improve communication skills, then we run the risk of issues developing.

When we think about issues at work, school, or even in our relationships, what is often the underlying issue? What often causes the most strife? You guessed it, poor communication. Misunderstandings, personality conflicts, lack of communication, and expectations not met are just some of the many issues that arise from poor communication. In this day and age, the use of technology has created its own set of issues with miscommunication. Whether it is a misinterpreted email or a text with abbreviations that cannot be deciphered, the number of times problems are caused with communication are far too many to even count. Improved communication skills can help us overcome many of these issues or avoid them altogether. Imagine the improved quality of life you could experience if you could simply communicate more effectively.

There are books, courses, and even college majors that focus on communication. There is no way this chapter can cover the content to that extent, so we are going to summarize important aspects that research says are key factors to improve communication skills. First and foremost, listen. This may sound simple, but listening means putting aside your own thoughts and giving your full attention to the person relaying the information. This includes hearing or receiving the information while understanding the feelings behind the shared content and not interrupting, judging, or showing negative emotions that would alter the opportunity to receive the information. This is important because it helps in developing empathy and compassion in students. When students learn to put themselves in someone else's shoes, it helps them understand other students' point of view or even the struggles they are facing.

Another key factor is communicating effectively. Whether it is formal or informal, verbal or nonverbal communication, you should know your purpose and have a goal in mind. Plan and know ahead of time what information you wish to convey. While there is a huge difference between types of communication, the purpose is to share information. Being able to do this efficiently and effectively will help to enhance communication. A final aspect deals with emotions. Be aware of your emotions as well as the emotions of the person with whom you are communicating. Emotions can cause us to not listen carefully, over react, shut down, get over excited, and not be able to communicate effectively. Our emotions can be easily recognized through verbal communication, but also often just as easily recognized through nonverbal communication. Recognizing and respecting those emotions is essential.

Effective communication requires active listening and focused speaking. How often have you gone to a restaurant and simply observed the room for a few minutes? What kind of conversations do you see? Typically you will see people engaged more in texting or checking the cell phones than conversing with the person sitting with them. When people are talking with one another, are they modeling effective communication skills? As with most things in life, there is an art and a science to communication. Whether it is the art of storytelling to draw people into your speech or whether it is being actively engaged in conversation (eye contact) with someone at the dinner table, there are many aspects of communication that need to be developed. In fact, one of the primary traits of a quality leader is the ability to communicate effectively.

Teaching children how to communicate effectively is one of the most important tasks of a parent or teacher. Failing to teach proper communication skills could socially limit a child for a lifetime. Without the tools to communicate effectively, children may be less willing to ask questions, engage in conversations, share their own ideas, and lack the self-confidence to lead. All of these will hamper their long-term success in school and the real world.

Traditionally in classrooms communication has been a one-way street where the teacher talks and the students listen. In fact, research shows that some students may go days or even weeks without answering a question in a class. If students aren't interacting and actively engaged in learning, then they are not being given the opportunity to enhance their own communication skills. When there is no engagement in the learning, the dynamic of the classroom changes and the teachers become the only ones communicating. If students do nothing more than sit in class and listen to someone lecture for the whole period, they become bored, disengaged, and often disruptive. The whole communication process is shut down.

Think about your own classroom. Who voices their thoughts and opinions? Do students have a chance to ask questions? Do students have a chance to stand in front of the class and practice public speaking? What about written communication, how is that taught or conveyed? Are students sending emails and if so, how is that communication different from writing a text or a thank you letter or a research paper? What about eye contact? What about body language? Is communication assessed within the content areas? Are discussions occurring about communication and are students being taught how to and not to communicate? Do students know when to use nonverbal versus verbal communication within your class? How do students communicate with you? How can you improve the communication to help your students be better prepared for the real world?

> ### Did you know?
>
> Parents spend only 3.5 minutes per week in meaningful conversation with their children. https://www.msu.edu/~jdowell/135/factoids.html

Personal Experiences and Stories

I (Julie) have seen how miscommunication can affect the classroom. I have had students misuse words so that the meaning comes out totally wrong, misspell words, say the wrong word, and so on. I could tell stories about students not listening to one another and countless arguments and misunderstandings. I have had students pass out while giving speeches. I have had students hard of hearing and students who have speech impediments as well as graphomotor disorders. I have taught ESL (English Second Language) students with severe language barriers. After 21 years of teaching the stories seem never ending. Just when I thought I had seen it all, I received an email this year where I experienced a whole new type of miscommunication.

Our school has adopted iPads and, as a science teacher, I am trying to go paperless. I email students and then the students turn in work via email back to me. A few weeks ago I had a student turn in his work and instead of signing his name, he typed this: "Your murderous friend that will one day hunt you down and decapitate you with his nails." While people reading this may think this is a threat, it was not. This came from the gentlest, mildest, nicest, quietest student that I teach. Imagine the shyest and sweetest student you teach. Now imagine getting this as the signature of the email sent to you. Needless to say I confronted the student and he was mortified! I could tell by the shade of red his face turned and the size his eyes grew that it was a total mistake. He sent me an email without changing his signature that he had used in an email to a friend where they were trying to come up with the funniest and grossest signature. After talking with him and his mother, we all decided that using this email was the perfect teachable moment. Not only did he learn a lesson about communication, so did the rest of the student body.

Some of the best examples of nonverbal communication are the British television series and movies starring Mr. Bean, which is played by actor Rowan Atkinson. The movie, titled *Bean*, is one of my favorite comedies of all time. Interestingly, the character almost never speaks and when he does speak it is usually just one or two words. In an entire movie, it would be surprising if he spoke more than 40 or 50 words. What makes the character so interesting is that 99 percent of his communication is nonverbal communication.

While he rarely utters a word, his nonverbal communication allows the audience to understand the plot and accomplish his goal of making them laugh as well. His gestures, facial expressions, and even his posture communicate exactly what he wants to say. In one example, Mr. Bean uses his facial expression and eyes to express his discomfort at the speed of the train's movement, which is also very funny. In another scene, he puts his fingers in his ears to show the need to block out the noise. Both of these are great examples of nonverbal communication, which were expressed clearly to the audience. Many of the older silent movie actors like Charlie Chaplin shared these same skills where they could communicate nonverbally using only facial expressions, eye movements, gestures, the use of settings, props, and the environment. They exemplify nonverbal communication.

Did you know?

Researchers indicate that 55 percent of communication is body language. Your body language speaks volumes! http://www.psychologytoday.com/blog/beyond-words/201109/is-nonverbal-communication-numbers-game

Ideas to Try

Recognizing the importance of communication in regards to the success of students in school and life beyond school is crucial. Here are some ideas that you can incorporate into the classroom that will not only allow you to model effective communication but provide opportunities for students to discuss and work on the skills as well.

- **Text, spoken word, and written word**: Students live in a world with technology and often the ways to communicate using that technology are very different from conversational speaking or formal writing. I (Julie) cannot tell you how many times I have been given a paper with LOL written on it or how many times I have read formal papers that sound just like the students' talk, slang and all. We should help them recognize that there are appropriate times for each of these types of communication. First it is essential to identify situations where each type of communication is important. One way to do this is to have the same amount of notecards written out as students in the class. On the notecards write formal written sentences, text communication language, and slang spoken terms. Have each student stand and read the card. Then have the students put the cards into three groups: formal writing, spoken words, and text. Lead a discussion about when it is appropriate to use each of these. Next have a discussion or even role play what would happen if the correct or incorrect type of communication happened in a specific situation. Finally, reflect and continue to touch back on this throughout the year as communication is occurring.

- **Silent movies**: Allow your students to create short movies or skits. Some of the students would be writers for the movie and would have to write how the students would demonstrate certain emotions like anger, boredom, happiness, surprise, and others. The students would perform the skit and the audience would try to identify what was going on in the skit and what emotions the actors were exhibiting. This is a fun and entertaining way to learn nonverbal communication.

- **Work on public speaking skills**: As discussed in Chapter 6, students don't need to be great orators to be effective but they need to practice their presentation skills. Help students develop skills such as eye contact, projecting their voice, capturing their audience's attention, etc. By developing this skill at an early age it will be easier for them to face interviews and job presentations.

- **Telling Stories**: Cut out pictures from magazines or newspaper and place them in a box. Take turns pulling out one picture and tell a story of what you think is happening in the picture. For older children, have the stories become more complicated. For younger children you can start with looking at the faces in the pictures and talking about what their facial expressions might tell you.

- **Nonverbal cues**: When students speak or present to class, work on their nonverbal cues. What are their facial features like? Are they smiling, sneering, frowning, nodding along, or squinting? All of these show distinct different reactions to what is being said. When they are speaking, are they looking directly into the eyes of your listeners? Eye contact shows respect and interest. (While this may be a cultural issue, be aware that in the real world most professionals prefer eye contact.)

- **Role playing**: Make up cards with different activities, which are age or grade appropriate. The cards can include activities such as: playing with a friend, sharing a toy, arguing with a friend, being afraid of something, feeling left out, etc. Let students take turns playing the different people in the situation so that they get a feel for how all of the people may feel and look at situations from different points of view. Discuss verbal/nonverbal cues as well as body language.

- **Confronting conflict** is a skill that effective leaders possess. No one necessarily enjoys confrontation and, in fact, most people avoid it, but it is essential to effective communication and it is a skill that needs to be developed. Practice scenarios in the classroom that can help students understand dealing with conflict. I have extensive experience with a program called Conflict Resolution and highly recommend implementation. It can be implemented beginning around age 10.

- **Remember the audience's agenda**: When you're preparing any form of important communication – a speech, a talk, or even an email – it's very easy to get caught up in your agenda – the things that you are eager to say. However, this may be at odds with your audience's agenda. What do they want from you? Do they even care about your topic? How long are they willing to give you their attention? These are important questions to a teacher in preparing a lesson, but also important concepts for students to learn. Especially when you consider we live in a "me" generation, where most students think of themselves first and don't give much thought to others. Help them understand that effective communication should be other focused as much as possible.

- **Virtues** cannot be thrown out the window when communicating! Be patient and listen. Respect what is being said or asked. Model these actions in the classroom and discuss them when students aren't being respectful or engaged. Help them understand it is about relating to others.

● **Give students a voice**: This can be done by allowing them to ask and answer questions, by having sharing time, time to give a speech or perform, and having time to socialize. Making communication a priority for the students where they have a voice shows that what they have to say matters. Find ways to allow them to practice their voice. For more on this, see Chapter 6.

Key Points to Remember

● Make public speaking a normal part of your class and students will become more comfortable speaking in front of groups. Reinforce key concepts like tone, rhythm, and body language when they speak.

● Work on communication skills when students are working in groups. Remind students of nonverbal cues and body orientation when in the group setting.

● Remind students to keep their audience in mind when speaking, presenting, or working on group projects. This will be invaluable to them when they enter the workforce.

● Help students develop skills to confront issues effectively. Remember to focus on the issues not emotions. This skill will help students speak up and correct issues before they become major problems. This is part of being proactive rather than reactive.

● Communication is best utilized when respect is at the forefront. Remember you are responsible for your actions and should always respond in a respectful manner, even if disagreeing.

● Help students learn to actively listen, such as make eye contact, asking questions for clarity.

● Perform skits where students learn to identify body language and emotions. Remember we communicate primarily nonverbally.

18 Instruct the Individual

" Everybody is a genius. But if you judge a fish by its ability to climb a tree, it will live its whole life believing that it is stupid."

Albert Einstein

Our Thoughts and Some Research Too

One problem with formal education is the desire to treat everyone the same. However, students are not the same. Students vary in gender, cultures, interests, socioeconomic status, and talents. If students are so different, why do we try to make them all fit the same mold? Especially when you consider that students have different motivations, needs, causes for misbehavior, and even different goals. Unfortunately with standardized tests as our measuring stick, and sweeping policies such as zero tolerance, education only sees students as a collective faceless whole and often unfortunately disregards the individual.

But as Dr. Deborah Gilboa suggests, "Treating each student in the class in the same way – same communication style, motivation techniques, rewards, and consequences – would be like treating every tree and flower in your garden in the same way. It's a quick way to get overwhelmed by weeds." This is an excellent analogy because when students don't have the opportunity to develop their personal strengths, and explore their passions, then they stop growing and never have the chance to bloom into their full potential.

This is where education can take a cue from the coaching world. Great coaches objectively analyze a player's strengths and weaknesses and find ways to utilize their strengths and minimize their weaknesses. Just like on a football team, each player has different talents and abilities. Teachers have to be coaches within the classroom and help students find and build on their ability. Not everyone is a quarterback, but if they were, there would be no one to throw to or block. Recognizing a person's strengths and building on them is key. Each individual athlete is different just as each student in the classroom is different. All have strengths and bring unique qualities to the team or class. Those qualities should be developed and encouraged to grow. This is why the best coaches coach the person, not just the athlete. The coach knows the running back is an athlete, but he also knows what is happening in the athlete's personal life. He teaches the athlete life skills, and connects with him so he will perform better off the field as well as on the field.

Athletes each play a specific role on a team. Even when practicing, different groups practice different skills. For example, on a baseball team the pitchers may be throwing in the bullpen while the outfielders are shagging fly balls. In football, the offense and the defense have two totally different sets of drills. Think about how a soccer goalie prepares compared to the striker. Make the connection to the classroom. Do you have students who play different roles? Can there be different ways to practice various skills?

When the athletes practice in small groups and focus on their own individual areas of expertise, don't they often succeed and reach a higher level of performance? The defense becomes a stronger and more effective defense because of the different instruction they are getting than the offense. The goalies learn how to successfully defend the goal because of their specific instruction. Again, transfer that mentality to the classroom. Is there a way to help students perform better in small groups along specific paths? Won't that help them reach the next level of performance as it does with athletes?

How can coaches and teachers get to know their athletes' and students' individual strengths and path of learning? This takes time and effort, simple as that. But do we always have that time? Do we have the energy to make that effort? If we want our students to excel, we have to make the commitment. If you do not make the effort to learn your students' strengths, then you are setting them up for failure. My older son plays baseball at a competitive level. He runs fast, which often equates him with an outfielder. This year his high school baseball coach put him at shortstop because he recognized he has excellent hand-eye coordination. He started his Varsity season at shortstop and has performed at a level that often surprises even him. He still plays centerfield, but he also plays other positions. The coach has found a way to let him practice different areas with different groups of players. Can you do that with students in the classroom? Can students be a part of more than one group?

Differentiated instruction is one way in which teachers can focus on individualized instruction. By differentiating instruction, a teacher should be able to have individual goals for each student and monitor the progress and individual achievement. This does not mean having different lesson plans for each student, but it does mean planning lessons that the students can participate in that meet their individual needs. Small groups and creating learning paths for students allows for individualized instruction.

The philosophy behind this approach is that each student is different, has different learning styles, and develops at a different rate. So even in a classroom of 20 or 30, each student has an individual plan or path. The path may include several other students that can work and grow together. The number of students on each path depends on the skills of each individual student. For example, remember how we discussed that boys tend to enjoy reading informational type literature versus fiction or non-fiction narrative? By having learning paths students can do more of what they enjoy compared to everyone being made to do the same thing. This one adaptation will benefit many of your students without adding time to your planning.

In order for this to work successfully, the teacher must have a strong discipline plan and have an excellent connection with each student. Small group work is often happening with students who are working on the same objectives and individual conferences are often a regular occurrence. From the outside, the classroom can appear active and even a little disorganized. But if one looks closer, all students are actively engaged and invested in their own learning process. This is because you are teaching the individual, who has specific interests, goals, and motivations.

The students know the expectations of each lesson or activity and also know the behavior that is expected. A perfect example of this happens with our Writer's Workshop model. Students are all writing towards the same goal of completing a published piece. But each individual student is working at his or her own pace. Some may be brainstorming or pre-writing. Others may be editing each other's papers. Individual conferencing is continually occurring throughout the class period as students reach that part of their own path. Students also have publishing stations where their path is finished and they celebrate and then take a new path towards a new experience.

Did you know?

Providing learning paths for students will enhance their level of learning.
http://www.glencoe.com/sec/teachingtoday/subject/di_meeting.phtml

Personal Experiences and Stories

I (Julie) have 72 students who walk in my classroom door every day to explore science concepts. Do I know them all as well as each other? No. But I do try to get to know the strengths and ability levels of each student. I start off the beginning of the school year with an interest inventory activity. Since I teach science, I do this with a scientific twist. Most teachers start with this type of activity, so we all try to make them meaningful to our own areas of interest. I actually take class time to let the students share answers; this helps to make them feel like what they wrote matters. It also lets me hear the inflection in their voices to see what truly stands out for them. While academics are a priority in my classroom, the students are what truly matter. When they know this is how I feel, then a relationship of trust and mutual respect begins to form. Then the learning can begin.

Often with labs there are different challenges that the students can obtain and they can work on various levels. For example, when building a roller coaster, groups can work together to accomplish different goals. The goals are often designed together through class discussion. This allows students to choose the path they feel will best challenge them. If they complete one path, they can always move on to the next. While giving major assessments there are times when two tests are available. One is more challenging than the other, but they are graded the same. For example, when we test the circulatory and respiratory systems the students can opt to write the terms in English or they can opt to write the scientific counterpart. An answer may either be trachea or windpipe. The students take different paths to learning based on their level of interest. For some students learning major body systems is a huge challenge in itself. For others the path is different and they need and want the additional challenge.

Our school makes the individual learner a priority. We have sent teachers to conferences and training sessions to learn more about differentiated instruction. Countless hours have been spent researching materials and programs that support differentiated instruction. Monies have been allocated for additional teachers to be placed within the classrooms to help create small groups. In our Lower School the math and reading programs have all been designed to allow fluid paths for students to take to achieve individual goals to experience growth and success. The gains and growth the students have made are due in large part to their differentiated instruction.

I (Brad) used to illustrate to my parents at open house each year how people can learn differently. I would put a random series of ten numbers (e.g. 2584913607) on an overhead and cover it up. As I was introducing myself to the parents, I would tell them to get out a pencil and piece of paper for a pop quiz. It was funny to see the looks of the parents as they prepared for their quiz. I would ask them to put the pencil on the desk and look at the board while I uncovered the numbers and asked them to memorize them in order. I showed them the numbers for exactly 30 seconds. Then I covered up the numbers and asked them to write down the series of numbers.

I gave them one minute to recall the numbers then I called for "pencils down." Then I would put the numbers back up on the screen and ask how many they got right. As parents laughed, they would admit to three correct, or six correct, and some even got them all correct. Then I would ask them how they memorized the numbers, which was the point of my exercise. I asked who memorized it similar to a social security number and several hands went up; you, I said, are my intellectuals and they laughed. I then asked who memorized them to music, like a jingle, and sure enough a few hands would rise, and I responded that you are my creative people, which also elicited a laugh. Then I asked, who memorized them like a phone number, and a few more hands were raised, to which I replied, and you are my social butterflies! Everyone laughed and then I went on to explain that we all have different ways of processing and learning information.

This was a teachable moment for the parents because I would go on to explain that just because you learn a certain way doesn't mean your child learns the same way, and the key is to find out how they best learn. I said, for instance, your child may really learn best when she is listening to the radio, but if she is making F's then that is probably not her learning style. After every open house, I would always have several parents approach me and thank me for a fun but informative presentation.

Another example of instructing the individual is a strategy that I (Brad) have used when I taught science. Each semester, I would have the students read a book and present to the class. I would give the students wide latitude in choosing a book of interest as long as they could connect it with science. After reading their book, I would then give them wide latitude in how they presented the information.

I would give them some basic guidelines for information that I wanted to see in their assignment, but otherwise, I left it up to them to present the project. Some students chose to write papers, others chose to present PowerPoints, some chose to tell a story about the book, and others decided to make a movie trailer for their book. Much like the activity I did with the parents at open house, students chose various means to present their book. I knew the intellectual students would be providing book reports, while creative students would be presenting movie clips or sing a song and the social students might tell a story or find some other method for delivering their assignment. The important point was that regardless of the method, the students completed assignments.

Did you know?

You should NOT create a different lesson plan for every student, just as a coach doesn't make a different practice plan for each player. http://www.glencoe.com/sec/teachingtoday/subject/di_meeting.phtml

Ideas to Try

- **Interest and learning style inventories**: These allow teachers to get to know the students better. This not only helps the students learn about themselves, but it also gives you an idea of where their strengths and challenges lie in regards to the classroom and how they learn. Create your own to make it personal to your class.

- **Give pre-tests**: This allows teachers to create small groups based on ability level and work with students on specific concepts. Pre-tests should be given at the beginning of each unit to keep groups fluid.

- **Small group work and activities**: This allows students to work together and also learn from one another.

- **Team work and individual work**: Be sure to balance this within the classroom. This allows success to occur within groups and individually.

- **Flexible pacing**: Do all students in your class learn the same material at the same time? Can you create flexible schedules that allow students to work at their own pace? If a student fails a test, should they just go on to the next content? Is there remediation? Do you offer extra help and allow students to reach the mastery level?

- **Alternate assessments**: Do you give everyone in the class the same format of test? Do you have to in order to assess the content? Have you ever thought of offering an oral exam as well as a written exam? Being able to assess content should occur in many different ways, including projects.

- **Independent studies**: Do you allow students to choose their own topics of study and work at their own pace to meet specific goals? This is an excellent way to meet the needs of each student.

- **Renaissance learning programs**: Accelerated Reader and Accelerated Math programs have never been better!

  - Accelerated Reader: the program now offers individualized vocabulary lists and individual goal setting based on results of STAR Reading testing and generated ZPDs. Students have their own personal, meaningful AR points goal based on their own ability level. Students can take personalized vocabulary quizzes, use the vocabulary lists to generate writing and grammar assignments, and read books of their own choice. The students in our classes also have sharing days where they teach each other vocabulary. Students maintain their own "word wall journal" and are amazed to see how their own individual vocabulary has increased yearly.

  - Accelerated Math Live: the program is updated and linked to National, State and Common Core standards. There are thousands of standards to choose from to meet the levels of your students. There are three main factors that stood out to us when adopting this program. One aspect is that students can see who is also working on the same objective and can then work in small groups that are fluid. Students click on a link and the names pop up of students within the same class who are on the same problem or objective. The second aspect is that the tutorials are linked directly with Khan Academy. Videos are just a click away on either an iPad or computer. The third aspect our teachers appreciate is the red flag feature. If a student has worked for a period of time and is struggling then the teacher receives a red flag notice and the student cannot go on without teacher intervention. This way the teacher is able to help the student and make sure the concept is mastered.

- **ixl.com**: Use this website to complement your math program. This program allows students to be self-paced as well as receive tutorials for concepts they do not understand. Note: this is a complement to your current program; it should not become your only program.

- **Utilize technology**: iPads and laptops can aid in differentiated instruction. There are apps that allow for videoing and voice recording. Notes can be taken in a whole different manner. Projects and assessments can be constructed using various programs and apps.

- **Flip the classroom**: Students can watch a brief lesson at home and then apply the information in class. That way you can observe and assess each student and help him or her as needed.

- **Use tactile, auditory, visual, and kinesthetic methods in teaching**: Vary the delivery method in which you teach your classes. Most teachers use auditory as the main delivery method in their classrooms while most students are not auditory learners.

Key Points to Remember

- Get to know the individual within the classroom. This can be done through sharing time, interest inventories, learning style inventories, journaling, and so on.

- Create opportunities for students to do individual activities and lessons. This can be a project, a book, writing, and by using tools such as Accelerated Reader, Accelerated Math, ixl.com, and more.

- Help students set individual goals and recognize when they have achieved them.

- Recognize different learning styles in your teaching and in the students within your class.

- Use techniques such as flipping the classroom and alternate assessments.

- Provide several learning options, or different paths to learning, which help students take in information and make sense of concepts and skills, but this doesn't mean creating different lesson plans.

- Provide appropriate levels of challenge for all students. Don't water down the content for some students but have high expectations for all of them.

- Provide options on how they complete assignments. Some may prefer to write a paper, while others may prefer to perform a skit. As long as they show knowledge of the information, let their individuality come through in the assignment.

19 | **Authenticate Relationships**

" Piglet sidled up to Pooh from behind. "Pooh!" he whispered. "Yes, Piglet?" "Nothing," said Piglet, taking Pooh's paw. "I just wanted to be sure of you.""

A.A. Milne

Our Thoughts and Some Research Too

When we talk about the most important things in life, family and friends are always on the top of that list. These relationships are what make life worth living. But do we really know how to cultivate those relationships? Just like in life, there are numerous types of relationships that have to be fostered and developed within a school community. First, think of all of the people that students come in contact with while at school: friends, enemies, acquaintances, teachers, administrators, policemen, coaches, guidance counselors, and staff workers. Now think of the type of relationship they would have with each of those groups. Do students have the tools needed to be able to interact with all of these people let alone develop a relationship? Helping students learn to build relationships in schools is the stepping stone for them to build relationships in the real world.

While the types of relationships that are developed with each of these groups of people are different from one another, there are two central themes fluid throughout: Open communication and respect. Communication is a two-way street that must entail both speaking and listening. A person must be able to know when to talk and when to listen. Both roles are equally important and knowing when or how to do either is often a challenge. Respect, whether it is self-respect or respect for another, is giving attention or showing high regard for the situation or person. While it is often said that respect has to be earned, it also has to be given. Modeling respect equates with receiving respect. If we can teach our students about communication and respect then they will more likely be able to develop relationships.

The level of relationships generated is also very different and this equates with the time and effort put towards the relationship. Anything worth having takes time and effort to maintain. This allows it to become a meaningful relationship. Not all relationships need to be meaningful; some are superficial and are just needed for a brief amount of time. While it is important at the time, it is not necessarily a relationship for life. Knowing how to identify these relationships is an important skill students need to have. There is no way students can put forth the amount of effort needed to maintain a meaningful, healthy relationship with every person the students encounter. It is physically and mentally not possible. Prioritizing is crucial. This will help to develop and maintain the relationships that mean the most.

There are several aspects to relationship building that should be fostered with each student within the school setting. Here is a list of some things to do and not to do when building relationships:

THINGS TO DO

- Build a connection – share an emotional experience or something that will allow a connection to be made.
- Embrace uniqueness – celebrate and learn about differences in people.
- Self-confidence – be yourself and recognize that you have good things to offer.
- Reach out to others – this will help you to gain confidence in communication and also show an interest in another person. Showing an interest equates with feeling valued.
- Maintain communication – keeping in touch will allow the relationship to grow and continue.
- Listen! Be patient – your time will come to talk.

THINGS TO NOT DO

- Don't be controlling – respect is essential to relationship building, so trying to control someone is not respecting who they are.

- Don't judge – embrace peoples' differences and accept them for who and what they are. You can decide whether or not the relationship is worth maintaining. A bad decision on one person's part does not make them a bad person.

- Don't try to change others – people have to be willing to change on their own.

If these skills are focused on in our schools then students will have the tools they need to be able to build and maintain relationships. This should start at an early age and continue all throughout their educational experience.

There are two relationships that are probably the most important to the students while in school. First is their relationship with their friends and the second is their relationship with their teacher. The friend relationships can impact their daily life and can spill over into the academic setting. That is one of the reasons it is crucial to teach students about relationship building. The relationship with the teacher can impact their entire educational experience. It can generate a love for learning or a hate for school. There is extreme power associated with each of these types of relationships. Again, reinforce why it is essential to address relationship building with the students.

Relationships with Friends

People crave the socialization and desire to fit into a specific group. This is a lot of pressure for a child. Put on top of that the pressure of maintaining those relationships and continuing to try to be part of a group or to be well liked by others. It is important for students to prioritize and choose the people with whom they want to make connections and develop relationships and identify the people with whom they are going to be more acquaintances. Not feeling like they fit in can be very traumatic for students. It can lead to social issues, bullying, and poor self-esteem. This all impacts the lives of the students, but it also carries over into the classroom.

Does everyone have to be friends? Friendship is a relationship that is based on concern and welfare for others. It focuses on aspects such as mutual caring, value, and trust with a connection to love (http://plato.stanford.edu/entries/friendship). To be a friend means that the person is willing to engage in a partnership. While students often wish to be friends with everyone, not everyone has to be friends. It is fine to not be friends with someone, but the key aspect is to still respect them. Not everyone shares the same interests or emotional experiences as others. By embracing these unique differences and respecting the individuals, when interaction and communication occurs students need to know how to be respectful and kind.

Teachers are Role Models for Relationship Building

Developing relationships with students is directly correlated with student success. The students need to feel valued and respected. By modeling this type of relationship it can help the students to learn how to develop their own relationships. First and foremost you need to get to know your students, which means first learning their names. While this may seem almost juvenile, it is very meaningful to the students. Studies show that greeting the students at the door and calling them by name increases retention rates at schools by a surprising rate. The students feel there is a personal relationship and want to continue attending that school. Getting to know the personal interests of the students also helps create a connection and build a relationship. Especially, when you consider that you may be one of the only adults with positive influences in some students' lives.

This can be done through interest inventories or just by taking the time to interact with the students. I (Julie) try to get to know something special about every student I teach. I have 70 students who walk through my door every day. I know which one has a horse named Polar Express, which one dove the reefs in Bora Bora over the holiday break, and which one swam the championship meet a few weeks ago. I take an interest in my students by asking questions and allowing time for them to share with me. Building these personal relationships means trust and trust means being willing to take chances and experience growth. I honestly feel that students within my class trust me, respect me, and feel safe taking chances they may not normally take on their own. This is all due to the relationships that we have built.

Without a positive teacher/student relationship the students will not have the desire to challenge themselves to reach the next level. A weak or negative relationship will detract from the learning process. Unfortunately, I have witnessed this throughout my years of teaching. At previous schools where I have taught, I have watched teachers yell at students and belittle them. I have seen teachers laugh with a class at a student just to be part of the "group" and not respect the personal feelings of the student who was asking a question. And sadly, I have watched students shut down and lose a love for learning.

Teachers have got to realize the power of the relationships and use it in a positive way.

Relationships that are built with parents, teachers, and other adults in the school are also role-modeling opportunities. The teacher, parents, and student are what I like to call an educational team. A healthy relationship between the parent and teacher is an important one for students to observe. The key aspect being observed is communication. By modeling effective communication, it allows them to see a professional relationship between adults that they can use as a model for when they enter the business world. This is also the same when students see relationships being modeled between teachers and administration. Do the adults involved respect one another? Do they embrace differences and communicate effectively? Students can easily pick up when one teacher is not a fan of another or when they have a certain feeling about an administrator. Does this model an appropriate relationship that is supposed to be built on respect? Our goal as teachers is to model meaningful relationships so students will have the tools to be able to build their own within the educational setting and then transfer that skill to the real world.

Did you know?

Building self-worth is the basis of being able to build a relationship. If we help students feel good about themselves then they are more likely to embrace others. http://www.pathwaytohappiness.com/writings-insecurity.htm

Personal Experiences and Stories

When I (Julie) began working on this book, I asked my children if there were any specific stories they wanted told. This is one that my older son insisted should be shared as an example of building a relationship. When he was 13, he had a science teacher name Judy Lycke. As the year progressed, she would often share stories about him with me that showed she took a personal interest in my son. She knew about his passion for baseball and it was obvious she cared about him beyond just his academic prowess. I attribute his success in the class with the bond that was built between student and teacher. She showed she cared about him. This made him more willing to take chances in his learning and helped him reach a higher level of education. He had the opportunity to have her as a teacher two years later and again performed at a level beyond expectations while having the utmost respect for Ms. Lycke as a teacher. Due to some personal goals my son has, he applied this year for a challenging course that most students take in their last year of high school. He knew if he made it in the course he would for the third year be sitting in Ms. Lycke's class. Needless to say, he made it. But unfortunately, this year my son has experienced some medical and health issues. Ms. Lycke has once again looked at him as a person, not just a student. She has conducted research on her own and helped reassure him about his condition. She has talked with him and helped him get through a tough time. When he found out some possible connections and treatment she was the person he went to and shared the information. This relationship has meant a lot to my son, and even more to us as parents. By my son having experienced this type of relationship, he is able to transfer that to communicating with other adults. He will be graduating high school next year and I feel that the modeling Mrs. Lycke has done has helped to prepare my son for developing professional relationships in the real world.

Did you know?

Relationships are never static. They are constantly evolving and we need to be able to grow and change with them. http://www.peace.ca/breakthroughexperience.htm

Ideas to Try

- **Learn and use names**: While this may seem simple, it is important to learn names of people. Teachers should model this to the students. Students should learn the names of their classmates and their teachers. This shows a level of respect. It is the basis for a possible relationship to develop. If someone is called the wrong name then it means the person does not care enough to learn the correct name. That in itself sends a message.

- **Develop students' self-worth**: People have to believe in their own self in order to be able to build a relationship. By providing a safe, comfortable environment, the students are more likely to be able to develop their own self-worth. The students need to know it is OK to fail and to ask questions. They need to feel like they are cared for and that they matter. From there, they can build on their self-worth and develop the skills to interact with one another. Developing self-worth can happen in numerous ways. Have students make a list of their good qualities and tape it someplace where they can see it regularly. Another activity I do is that I have all of the students put their name on the top of a sheet of paper. We then pass the paper around student by student until every student has written on everyone's paper. The goal is to write one positive thing about that person and sign your name to it. By the end the student has a paper full of positive attributes. This not only helps to build self-worth, it also helps to build relationships.

- **Learn what is happening outside of the classroom**: When a teacher knows the situations happening outside of the classroom then she is more likely to have empathy for what happens inside the classroom. In fact, they view these "outside problems" as an opportunity to further build a relationship with both the students and the parents. This can make all of the difference in the world to the student's success in the classroom. In past years, I have had students whose parents have gone through divorces, who have experienced deaths in the family, and have had serious illnesses. This impacts performance in the classroom, and by me being aware of these situations, I was able to help the students cope with their school responsibilities on an individual level and build a meaningful relationship with both the student and parents.

- **Use your resources**: Guidance counselors are an amazing resource to use in relationship building. Include them in lessons and use them as resources for the students. By students seeing them as a safe and trusted resource, they are more likely to go to them if needed. This includes when they are out in the real world and may need help or advice.

- **Set boundaries for students**: Rules and regulations are a key aspect in a safe learning environment. First recognize all school rules that need to be followed. From there involve your students in every way possible to generate other rules. If they have a say then they will also have buy-in. Post the rules and refer to them whenever necessary. Consequences should be meaningful and also agreed upon by the students. Buy-in is key. In our school we have an honor code statement that students write and sign before any major assessment. We also have an opportunity for students to be a part of an honor council. Because of the respect for the honor system at our school, the students know they are in a safe setting and are able to build relationships within that setting. Modeling this type of setting will help students recognize safe settings in the future.

- **Give students time to interact**: There are countless ways for students to interact with one another. Before the interaction occurs, review the virtues of respect and communication. Be sure to have a safe learning environment to help foster relationships.

  Here are a few ideas:

  - Group work including cooperative learning lessons and jigsaw lessons
  - Team-building activities and teamwork lessons
  - Partner reads
  - Peer editing
  - Lab groups and projects
  - Free time such as recess and scheduled sharing time

- **React appropriately to questions and situations**: The way we react to situations shows how we respect the others involved in the situations. I have seen numerous times when students have asked questions that have just been silly or what others students thought were just plain stupid questions. These questions are usually accompanied by the laughing of one or several students. Never have I laughed along with the class. The student asking the question trusted me enough that he felt safe enough to ask a question. Laughing at him would have destroyed any relationship that we had established. While I may have been shaking my head on the inside, never would I laugh or react negatively on the outside. Instead, I answer the question in a meaningful way and make sure the student still feels respected. This also sends a message to the other students and they know I would treat them the same way. It strengthens all of the relationships in the class. This type of modeling of respect is important for students to see. Hopefully they will be able to make connections when with their friends and in the same type of situation.

- **Build a culture of respect**: Respect is a theme that runs throughout all aspects of life itself. By modeling and promoting respect within the classroom, the students are more likely to model respect themselves and promote it with others. Respect is the basis of healthy and meaningful relationships. Without respect there is no relationship. I try to make connections to the real world whenever possible. In science class we talk about respecting nature and how we have a relationship with the environment. We also talk about respecting each other and our relationships with one another. Group projects, labs, and cooperative grouping cannot successfully be completed if we do not work together and respect one another.

- **Writing about relationships**: Have students write poems or keep journals to share their thoughts about relationships. Here is an example of some similes students wrote to express how they feel about relationships from http://www.thechangeblog.com/how-to-make-friends:

  - Relationships are like fences. They can keep you together.
  - Relationships are like school. You can learn from them.
  - Relationships are like the stars, when they are out in the open.

Key Points to Remember

- Relationships are built on respect and communication.
- Teachers are powerful role models in regards to relationships.
- Recognize, share, and focus on key traits that make for a meaningful relationship all throughout the school year.
- Recognize that relationships can be different with different people.
- Create a sense of comfort and safety for students within your classroom. This includes building trust and having rules and regulations that are consistently reinforced.
- Know and share the support resources available in schools.

20 | Merge the Real World into the Classroom

"Formal learning can teach you a great deal, but many of the essential skills in life are the ones you have to develop on your own."

Lee Iacocca

Our Thoughts and Some Research Too

Teachers all have personal and professional goals. Some may include reaching every student, making the classroom exciting and fun, instilling creativity, or communicating better with parents, while others may be to further a degree or earn a different teaching position. The list of goals can be very expansive, but we must agree that one goal all teachers have in common is to prepare the students to be members of society. In their first year of school this goal looks very different from their final years at a university. The first year we are teaching the students to read and write. This will help them to interact at their current developmental level within the community they live. While in the final years of high school or at a university the goal should be to help the student become self-sufficient, responsible, and independent. We want to help our students experience success and learn how to ultimately become productive members of society.

This is where merging the real world into the classrooms is essential. The sooner the students are introduced to real-world issues, professions, and life in general, the sooner they can figure out how to become a productive member within that community or culture. We as teachers need to take every opportunity possible to bring real-life, meaningful situations to the attention of our students. This should be thoughtfully and seamlessly integrated within the curriculum at every grade level.

While we recognize the importance of learning the basics and having a solid educational foundation, we also want to recognize other skills that are needed in the workplace. You will not even be hired for a position if you are not qualified. The academic background knowledge is essential to getting your foot in the door. But once you are in the workplace there are skills that go beyond the academic content. Students need to learn problem-solving skills, responsibility, teamwork, communication skills, flexibility, and adaptability. They also need to know how to think critically and be open-minded. Most of these topics are not the focus within the classroom. This is mainly due to standardized tests and accountability standards that the schools must adhere to. Any additional "fluff" is not welcome in the classroom because the time needs to be spent mastering mathematical content and reading more proficiently. What teachers need to understand is that both can happen. Integrating the real-world scenarios into the academic curriculum actually strengthens the curriculum and brings meaning to learning the material.

The path that students take with their educational career should not impact the goal of preparing the students for the real world. There are some communities where college is expected and others where it is not often pursued. Sometimes paths are chosen for people due to financial restraints or other obligations. Not everyone comes from an affluent family where they can take over the family business or have a trust fund to attend an Ivy League university. Not every student's parents attended college and have advanced, professional degrees. Those scenarios represent the minority of the students that are currently in our education system. The truth is that the world population is about 7 billion and only about 7 percent of the world's population has a college degree.

In October 2012 the U.S. Bureau of Labor Statistics reported that 66.2 percent of high school graduates enrolled in colleges or universities. That also means that 33.8 percent did not attend college. The unemployment rate for high school graduates not enrolled in college was 34.4 percent. The statistics also state that between the year 2011 and 2012 370,000 American students dropped out of high school.

So what does this all mean? First of all the high school graduates attending colleges will be given opportunities to choose a major and study towards a career of their choice. This hopefully will give them real life experience even with the possibility of internships. This exposure is invaluable, but still does not guarantee a job upon graduation. Numerous graduates have to take a job outside of their area of study because of such a competitive job market. Many companies now are even requiring advanced degrees beyond the bachelor's degree. This can be competitive and stressful. Are the students prepared for that? Isn't that why they went to college in the first place? Most graduates assume they are guaranteed a job upon graduation. Sadly, that is often not the case. There are students who graduate with no job and are in debt. What do they do? Did schools prepare them for that scenario?

What about the students who do not attend college and are unemployed? Are they prepared for real life? Do they even know what professions are available within their own communities? Were they ever exposed to that type of information? What are their options? Do they know how to apply for a job? Are they aware of other options besides college? Did their schools educate them on all of their options once they graduate?

Vocational, Trade and Tech Schools are becoming increasingly popular as the demand for skilled jobs is on the rise. These schools have online programs as well as campus programs. The length of time to complete a program varies but usually ranges from 9 months to 2 years. A 2012 salary study by Industry Week found that manufacturing managers earned an average salary of $99,643 per year and the median for the workers within the factory was $86,000. The so-called "blue-collar" job that was once looked down upon now is looking pretty enticing to many. Would students even know about these options beyond high school? Do they know the hundreds of different professions that can be learned by attending these types of institutions? Was this a part of their education while in school?

What about the high school dropouts? Are they prepared with the skills to be productive members of society? Even better than that, were they made aware of the consequences if they did drop out? Do schools educate the students on their possible futures based on choices that are made now? Shouldn't that be a discussion to be had within the classrooms? Once students are out of school then who becomes their source of information? Do the students just feel their way through society and hope they get a job? Do some count on government help because they don't know what other options they have?

This is where the school systems can make a difference and create a meaningful education by merging the real world into the classrooms and educating the students not only on the basics, but life, integrating the basics with being a productive member of society.

> **Did you know?**
>
> Walt Disney dropped out of school at age 16, Bill Gates dropped out of college, Thomas Edison only attended regular schools for 3 months, and Elton John dropped out at age 16. http://people.howstuffworks.com/15-notable-people-who-dropped-out-of-school.htm

Personal Experiences and Stories

Every year our first grade students dress up as the professional that they want to be when they grow up. They share a brief presentation with the class about the profession and then an individual picture is taken. The pictures are all put on a poster and each parent can receive one. My older son dressed up as a doctor while my younger son first wanted to be a judge and then last minute decided professional musician was lots more fun! I do have to admit most students dress up to mimic their parents, but even when that happens the students are introduced to different professions at a very early age.

When students enter third grade in our school they learn the hard truth about being taxed. The lesson goes right along with taxation without representation and students are taxed for various reasons: some fair and some not so fair. This included things from sharpening pencils to going to recess. Every third grader rallied together during recess to denounce the unfair taxes imposed upon them by the ruling body of the third grade teachers. Students even all got on a ship on the playground and chanted, "No more taxes!" This activity once again shows the students what life is or was like in the real world.

What about partnering with members of the community? Our fourth and fifth grade students have helped build a nature trail at our school. Their contributions have been to design various stations throughout the trail. Part of the design consists of meeting with members of the community and local businesses. They go on field trips to visit the businesses or have guest speakers come in the classroom. The students also gather information and purchase their materials that they need just like they were running their own business. This interaction with people who have real jobs in areas of interest for the students gives them a meaningful connection to real life beyond the walls of the school.

And isn't it ironic that students all want to have different careers or vocations? Just as many teachers say they knew they wanted to teach at a young age, I know many firemen, first responders, police, and other fields where people said they knew at a young age that that was the career they wanted. Remember every student has talents and strengths and that is a good thing. This means they can identify and build upon their strengths to excel in the real world.

What if every student went to college and got a teaching degree? Where would they all work? They all couldn't be teachers. So the notion that everyone should be working toward the exact same goal is senseless. I remember a student several years ago who was a good football player who in fact was being recruited by some colleges to play football. However, he wanted to be an EMT (Emergency Medical Technician) and had wanted to be one since he was a child. An EMT had spoken to his class during a career day and had talked about how he had saved people's lives and how much he loved making a difference.

While college could have possibly given him even more opportunities, it was not what he desired to do. While some questioned the fact that he had limited his opportunities, he knew what he wanted to do. After high school, he enrolled for his EMT training and has been an EMT for a couple of years and loves his career helping others. When students realize their strengths, passions, and the potential they have then they can enter the world with the skills to excel, regardless of their chosen vocation.

Did you know?

The most popular careers are not associated with the highest salary. They are chosen because people have a healthy working environment, feel challenged, and respected. http://www.huffingtonpost.co.uk/2014/03/17/happiness-is-more-important-than-money_n_4978127.html

Ideas to Try

- **Guest speakers**: This is the easiest and often most valuable way to bring in people from the "real world" into the classrooms. This can be done with any subject area that is taught. Think about how cool the class will be if taught by the local weatherman or having flutes handmade with a local musician. That describes two specific experiences our students get in fourth and fifth grade. Having that outside connection with a "professional" often increases the level of interest, which ultimately raises the level of learning.

● **Mimic a professional when possible**: Track a hurricane or give a weather forecast when you study weather, become editors when writing papers, experience scientific labs through the eyes of a scientist or inventor. Making that specific connection to things you already do in class can easily be done and has an everlasting impact on the students.

● **Job fair**: While this takes a good bit of preparation on many people's part, the benefit for the students is well worth it! My (Julie) husband owns his own physical therapy clinic in the area and he was invited into a school for a job fair. This was done for a group of 10-year-olds at a public school to show them local businesses and to help the students learn what it takes to work at each. In attendance were jobs such as a lineman for a local electrical company, a karate instructor, IT opportunities, and clowns and entertainers. This job fair fit the population of the school. The key factor was local professions. When designing a job fair be sure to know the goal of the population attending the fair.

● **Give a career survey**: Let the students take a career survey to find out their areas of interest. This will give them more information and possible ideas for professions that they may not think about. Often students equate professions or getting a job with making money. Their first instinct is not to follow a passion, but to earn money. A career survey will help them look through the lens of their passion.

● **Solve real-world problems**: There are so many problems that occur everyday around the world. Give the students the opportunity to be problem solvers. This can be to redesign a device or solve a government issue. The ideas are endless. In fifth grade we realized food waste is a huge issue that not only wastes the food, but also the money being spent on the food. Together the students came up with a goal and program to help minimize food waste during our school lunches. Included in this was a field trip to the composting center and meetings with the cafeteria staff. Again, the real-world connection. This type of activity enhances problem-solving skills, teamwork, communication skills, flexibility, and adaptability.

● **Hold a debate**: In our science class my 10-year-olds are split into three groups with the goal of having a debate. They are posed with a fictitious situation where Disney is buying a piece of land and going to build an amusement park. One group represents Disney, another the neighborhood homeowners, and a third a nature conservancy who wants to protect the land. They each have to present a case to a panel of judges and fight for their cause. The students learn so much from this activity! They learn how debates work and they recognize that there is more than one viewpoint in every situation.

- **Modeling and role play**: Have you ever been a member of parliament? What about a judge? Can you present and defend a court case to your peers? Can you imagine a classroom where the teacher models a dictator? What about having an elected Senior and Junior Council who can propose legislature to the dictator? What about having a Censor who hands out discipline consequences? Have you ever dressed up as someone famous? All of these are examples of various activities that happen within our History classes. The students role play and experience professions from the past and present. They step into the persona of someone famous and experience their careers and important events within their lives. This is not limited to History. In English class the students become book critics and authors, in science they become inventors and scientists.

- **Provide team-building opportunities**: Allow students to work as a team to successfully complete a task. This can be within an educational setting such as with a group project or lab or it can be something like a High Ropes program. Be sure to allow students time to experience challenges and work them out as a team. They need to experience problem solving, flexibility, and adaptability. They will also need to practice their communication skills and be responsible for their own actions. Also be sure students are able to bring their own strengths into the team atmosphere. Finally, allow for reflection. This will help to analyze the experience, to learn, and grow from it.

- **Service opportunities**: Schools with service learning programs help their students to be immersed within real life settings where people benefit from their help. This allows students to grow on so many different levels. It also helps them to understand their own community, different communities, and other cultures.

- **Find websites and fun ways to bring the real world into the classroom**: I like the site http://www.bls.gov/k12 for bringing kid-friendly information into the classroom. This is a creative way to get students interested in learning information that is provided by the US Department of Labor

Services. There are age-appropriate activities for all grade levels that help students find careers based on their own interests and learn about the economy. I also like the site http://kids.usa.gov/teens-home/jobs/index. shtml to help students learn about careers and various professions. There are short videos available to see real people at work actually doing the different professions. This is also developmentally age appropriate.

Key Points to Remember

- Merging the real world into the classroom can happen at any age and grade level.

- Find meaningful ways to bring in professionals, guest speakers, or incorporate careers into the academic content areas.

- Keep in mind the students' interests when bringing in guest speakers and introducing professions.

- Be sure to expose students to service opportunities.

- Provide team-building opportunities to work on skills needed beyond the world of academia.

- Encourage students to become the best "self" they can be regardless of their interests. Remember if all students are able to develop to their full potential, then they will be happier and more successful in the real world. It is never too early to build the foundation of skills needed for success and the pursuit of excellence.

Bibliography

Adaptability and flexibility. Retrieved from http://www.kent.ac.uk/careers/sk/adaptability.htm

Barbour, A. (2000) *Louder than words: Nonverbal communication.* Retrieved from https://openlibrary.org/books/OL5205625M/Louder_than_words_...

Berger, Elizabeth, M.D. (nationally recognized child psychiatrist) in discussion with the author (Brad Johnson), April 2014.

Biro, M. (2013) 5 Reasons why workplace flexibility is smart talent strategy. *Forbes.* Retrieved from http://www.forbes.com/sites/meghanbiro/2013/08/18/5-reasons-why-workplace-flexibility-is-smart-talent-strategy

Booher, D. (2010, August 27) Gender negotiation communication style differences: Women. Retrieved from http://www.negotiations.com/articles/gender-bender

Borba, M. (2009) *The big book of parenting solutions: 101 answers to your everyday challenges and wildest worries.* New York: Jossey-Bass.

Brady, S. (2010, September 3) World's worst cultural mistakes. Retrieved from https://travel.yahoo.com/ideas/worlds-worst-cultural-mistakes-011841671.html

Branzei, S. (2002) *Grossology.* New York: Penguin Putnam.

Bronson, P. & Merryman, A. (2014) *Top dog: The science of winning and losing.* New York: Twelve.

Coloroso, B. (1994) *Kids are worth it! Giving your child the gift of inner discipline.* New York: Avon Books.

Cookson, J. (2011, November 3) How U.S. graduation rates compare with the rest of the world. Retrieved from http://globalpublicsquare.blogs.cnn.com/2011/11/03/how-u-s-graduation-rates-compare-with-the-rest-of-the-world.

Covey, S. (1991) *Principle-centered leadership.* New York: Free Press.

— (2011) *The 6 most important decisions you'll ever make: A guide for teens.* New York: Touchstone.

Cowie, C (2010, August 29) *Gender language.* Retrieved from http://www.lingutronic.de/Studium/Anglistik/Gender%20Language/Gender%20Language.pdf

Deborah Gilboa, M.D. (international parenting expert) in discussion with the author (Brad Johnson), April 2014.

Diane Johnson (V.P. of Human Resources, Kraft Foods) in discussion with the author (Julie Sessions), March 2014.

Donaldson, G. (2001) *Cultivating leadership in schools: Connecting people, purpose, and practice.* Williston, VT: Teachers College Press.

Doug Bergman (Google certified technology instructor) in discussion with the author (Julie Sessions), February 2014.

Dykhuizen, G. (1973) *The life and mind of John Dewey* (J. A. Boydston, Ed.). Carbondale: Southern Illinois University Press.

Gabriel, J. G. (2005). *How to thrive as a teacher leader.* Alexandria, VA: Association for Supervision and Curriculum Development.

Goldberg, A. (2014) What makes a great coach? Retrieved from https://www.competitivedge.com/special-%E2%80%9Cwhat-makes-good-coach%E2%80%9D

Grant, A. (2014, April 11) Raising a moral child. Retrieved from http://www.nytimes.com/2014/04/12/opinion/sunday/raising-a-moral-child.html

Jarc, R. (2009, October 29) Character study reveals predictors of lying and cheating. Retrieved from http://josephsoninstitute.org/surveys/#sthash.DlOk8UaL.dpuf

Johnson, B. & McElroy, T. (2010) *The edutainer: Connecting the art and science of teaching.* New York: Rowman & Littlefield.

Klaus, P. (2007). *The hard truth about soft skills: Workplace lessons smart people wish they'd learned sooner.* New York: Harper Collins.

Kraus, Amanda (Executive Director of Row New York) in discussion with the author (Brad Johnson), January 2014.

Long, K. (2013) Games to keep teenage girls enthralled with math, science. Retrieved from http://seattletimes.com/html/localnews/2021302993_girlgamexml.html

Manari, Christen (Eduspire Ipad Instructor) in discussion with the author (Brad Johnson), April 2014.

Max Planck Institute for Evolutionary Anthropology (2010, August 27). Dogs can read thoughts. Retrieved from http://www.mpg.de/204744/Dogs_social_cognition

McManus, B. (2010, August 27) Gender and modes of communication. Retrieved from http://www2.cnr.edu/home/bmcmanus/gendercom.html

Meaningful relationships. Retrieved from http://www.counseling.txstate.edu/resources/shoverview/bro/meaningfulrel.html

Must have leadership skills for the 21st century. Retrieved from http://westsidetoastmasters.com/article_reference/must_have_leadership_skills_for_21st_century.html

National Center for Education Statistics (2012) Dropouts, completers and graduation rate reports. Retrieved from http://nces.ed.gov/ccd/pub_dropouts.asp

NOVA (2010, August 30) Dances with bees. Retrieved from http://www.pbs.org/wgbh/nova/bees/dancesdark.html

Parker-Pope, T. (2009, February 24) The 3 R's? A fourth is crucial, too: Recess. *New York Times*. Retrieved from http://www.nytimes.com/2009/02/24/health/24well.html?_r=0

Rath, T. (2007) *Strengths finder 2.0 report*. New York: Gallup Inc.

Robinson, K. (2012, December 7) Do schools kill creativity? Retrieved from http://www.huffingtonpost.com/sir-ken-robinson/do-schools-kill-creativity_b_2252942.html

Sarah Davis (leadership consultant) in discussion with the author (Brad Johnson), March 2014.

Sawyer, R. (2012) *Explaining creativity: The science of human innovation*. New York: Oxford.

Sears, N. (n.d.) Building relationships with students. *NEA*. Retrieved from www.nea.org/tools/29469.htm

Silby, Caroline, Ph.D. (nationally recognized sports pyschologist) in discussion with the author (Brad Johnson), March 2014.

Snow, C. & Shattuck, L. (n.d.) *Improving reading outcomes: Getting beyond third grade*. Retrieved from http://www.ecs.org/clearinghouse/26/49/2649.htm

Sykes, L. (2009, December 31) Move over boys: More girls playing video games. Retrieved from http://abclocal.go.com/kabc/story?id=7196100

Tardanico, S. (2012, November 29) 5 habits of highly effective communicators. *Forbes*. Retrieved from http://www.forbes.com/sites/susantardanico/2012/11/29/5-habits-of-highly-effective-communicators

Torrance, P. (1993) Understanding creativity: Where to start? Retrieved from http://www.jstor.org/discover/10.2307/1448974?uid=2&uid=4&sid=21103982534407

Willis, J. (2006) *Research-based strategies to ignite student learning: Insights from a neurologist and classroom teacher.* Alexandria, VA: Association for Supervision and Curriculum Development.

Woollaston, V. (2013) How often do you check your phone? Retrieved from http://www.dailymail.co.uk/sciencetech/article-2449632/How-check-phone-The-average-person-does-110-times-DAY-6-seconds-evening.html

Yettick, V. (2014, April 22) U.S. 4th graders get more help with less homework, study finds. *Education Week*. Retrieved from http://blogs.edweek.org/edweek/inside-school-research/2014/04/international_homework.html

Sources for Epigraphs

Introduction

Einstein, A. Retrieved from https://www.goodreads.com/quotes/19914-it-is-in-fact-nothing-short-of-a-miracle-that

Chapter 1

Nader, R. Retrieved from http://www.brainyquote.com/quotes/quotes/r/ralphnader110188.html

Chapter 2

Disney, W. Retrieved from http://www.brainyquote.com/quotes/quotes/w/waltdisney131648.html

Chapter 3

Seuss, Dr. (1978). *I Can Read with My Eyes Shut*! Random House Childrens Books. Retrieved from https://www.goodreads.com/quotes/6806-the-more-that-you-read-the-more-things-you-will.

Chapter 4

Einstein, A. Retrieved from http://www.brainyquote.com/quotes/a/alberteins122147.html

Chapter 5

Dewey, J. Retrieved from http://www.experientialtools.com/about/experiential-education/

Chapter 6

Covey, S. Retrieved from http://www.stephencovey.com/blog/?p=16

Chapter 7

Caldwell, T. Retrieved from http://www.brainyquote.com/quotes/t/taylorcald186293.html.

Chapter 8

Ward, W.A. Retrieved from http://www.brainyquote.com/quotes/w/williamart110017.html

Chapter 9

Gandhi, M. Retrieved from https://www.goodreads.com/quotes/77091-it-is-wrong-and-immoral-to-seek-to-escape-the

Chapter 10

Merritt, J. (2012) *Still Standing: 8 Winning Strategies for Facing Tough Times*. Eugene: Harvest House Publishing.

Chapter 11

Diller, P. Retrieved from http://www.brainyquote.com/quotes/p/phyllisdil125353.html

Chapter 12

Emerson, R. W. Retrieved from http://www.brainyquote.com/quotes/r/ralphwaldo134859.html

Chapter 13

Einstein, A. Retrieved from https://www.goodreads.com/quotes/8547S-the-measure-of-intelligence-is-the-ability-to-change

Chapter 14

Roosevelt, T. Retrieved from http://www.brainyquote.com/quotes/t/theodorero147876.html

Chapter 15

Mead, M. Retrieved from http://www.brainyquote.com/quotes/m/margaretme100502.html

Chapter 16

Jackson, P. Retrieved from https://www.goodreads.com/quotes/52132-the-strength-of-the-team-is-each-individual-member-the

Chapter 17

Robbins, T. Retrieved from http://www.brainyquote.com/quotes/t/tonyrobbin147783.html

Chapter 18

Einstein, A. Retrieved from https://www.goodreads.com/quotes/101458-everybody-is-a-genius-but-if-you-judge-a-fish

Chapter 19

Milne, A. A. (1928/2009) *The House at Pooh Corner*. Egmont. Retrieved from http://thinkexist.com/quotation/piglet-sidled-up-to-pooh-from-behind-pooh-he/354777.html

Chapter 20

Iacocca, L. Retrieved from http://izquotes.com/quote/320688